STARTERS
&DESSERTS

STARTERS & DESSERTS

CAROL BOWEN & LOUISE STEELE

ELIZABETH AYRTON · ELAINE BASTABLE
KATHARINE BLAKEMORE · PATRICIA BOURNE
ARABELLA BOXER · JACKIE BURROW
EMMA CODRINGTON · CAROLINE ELLWOOD
DEH-TA HSIUNG · HEATHER LAMBERT
PRUE LEITH · MICHAEL RAFFAEL
ROSEMARY STARK · ROSEMARY WADEY
PAMELA WESTLAND · JENI WRIGHT

CONTENTS

First published in 1987 by Octopus Books Limited
Grosvenor Street, London, England

© 1987 Hennerwood Publications Limited

ISBN 0 86273 396 0

Printed in Great Britain

INTRODUCTION

Choosing a meal's main course is usually quite straightforward: depending on the season, who you are cooking for and your own inclination, you will want something hot and hearty – an aromatic casserole of meat, poultry or game, perhaps, a hearty fish pie or a splendid joint of meat – or something cool and refreshing like a delicately flavoured, elegantly presented whole salmon, a summery salad or a chicken cooked with fresh herbs. But what to put round the centrepiece you have decided on? How to lead up to the main course in fine style and with the right taste on the tongue and then bring the meal to a triumphant conclusion with the perfect pudding?

This book answers such questions. It provides a mouth-watering collection of over 160 recipes for stylish starters and delicious desserts, with numerous accompanying sauces and dressings and with interesting variations on many of the basic recipes. It also offers a wealth of helpful hints on how best to combine them, with main course dishes and with each other, to make a good range of well-balanced menus, from everyday meals for the family to special-occasion dinner parties.

Many of the recipes are for old favourites, whose combinations of ingredients and flavours ensure them a delighted welcome at every table, while others have been created specially for this book. You will find such classics as Spinach Soup, Pâté de Campagne, a smoked fish soufflé and an egg mayonnaise among the six chapters of starters and Summer Pudding, Crème Caramel, Bakewell Tart, Bread and Butter Pudding and Spotted Dick among the desserts; you will also be introduced to many new delights, including a 'nouvelle cuisine' version of chicken liver pâté, a wonderfully light Crab and Shrimp Terrine, crêpes with a tangy filling based on chicken, lemon and walnuts, a delicious sorbet of tropical fruits including mango and passion fruit, a richly coffee-flavoured Mocca Soufflé and a splendid Rhubarb Crumble Flan.

You will find the recipes grouped in twelve handily titled sections – six of starters and six of desserts – to help you home in quickly on exactly the type of recipe you are looking for. The starters include good selections of soups and pâtés, savoury dishes, recipes based on many kinds of fish, first-course vegetables and salads and pasta, rice and pancake dishes. The desserts sections are just as wide-ranging, traditional puddings contrasting with trifles and mousses, ices and sorbets, and pies and flans vying for attention with gâteaux, cheesecakes and fruit-based desserts. To help in planning ahead, all recipes include preparation times with notes indicating the need for any lengthy processes like soaking, cooling or freezing: no need to exhaust yourself trying to prepare a three-course meal in the two or three hours before the food is to be served when the work could be planned in advance and carried out over two or three days. Since presenting dishes to look their best is also important, many suggestions for garnishes and decorations have been included, both in the recipes themselves and in the chapter introductions. Each recipe is photographed in colour.

Soups

Thick, chunky and nourishing; smooth and creamy; light and colourful; chilled and reminiscent of summer: there is a delicious soup for any occasion.

Soups have no seasonal boundary, though you could opt, if you like, for a light vegetable soup in early spring; an oriental bean-sprout and vegetable recipe on long hot summer days; a rich colourful and spicy pumpkin soup during autumn; or a hearty and warming French onion soup for winter.

The basis for every tasty soup is a good home-made stock and time taken preparing a batch will pay healthy dividends on flavour. Once made, serve your soup at the ideal temperature. Vegetable soups and broths are best served piping hot; creamy chowders and dairy-based soups taste delicious on the warm side of hot; and vichyssoise, gazpacho and other chilled soups should be served almost icy cold.

For presentation, some soups need little more than a generous sprinkling of chopped parsley or freshly snipped herbs. Other, often plainer, offerings need more imaginative garnishes. Experiment with plain or seasoned, cubed or shaped croûtons; shredded, grated or cut-out pieces of vegetables and cheese; lavish swirls of cream, yogurt or plain fromage frais; a dusting of spices, cheeses or toasted bread-crumbs, or an exotic lattice of shredded omelette, arrangements of radish discs, scattering of nuts or seeds or colourful array of citrus zest curls.

The lighter vegetable soups in this chapter make wonderful starters for hearty meat and game main courses like Boeuf Bourguignon, Duck Breasts with Orange Sauce and Guard of Honour. Thicker, more substantial soups are perfect with baked whole fish like sea bass or carp and easy-on-the-waistline chicken dishes such as Chicken Provençal, poached chicken in a lemon sauce or a quick chicken and vegetable stir-fry dish.

Finish the lighter starter menus with equally light desserts like a meringue vacherin, a wafer-thin pastry fruit flan or fruit poached in a liquor-laced syrup, such as Pears in Grenadine. Heartier soup, starters and lighter main course menus can afford the luxury dessert treatment – opt for rib-sticking sponges, pastries with custard or indulgent chocolate treats.

From the top: Spinach Soup (page 16), Carrot and Lentil Soup (page 19)

LIGHT VEGETABLE SOUP

Preparation time: 30 minutes
Cooking time: 30 minutes

1 knob butter
1 small onion, peeled and finely chopped
175 g (6 oz) carrots, scrubbed and cut into narrow matchstick strips
3 celery sticks, trimmed, scrubbed and finely sliced
1 teaspoon cornflour
900 ml (1½ pints) Vegetable stock (see below)
1 teaspoon tomato purée
2 tablespoons chopped fresh parsley
Omelette garnish:
2 eggs
salt
freshly ground black pepper
15 g (½ oz) butter
celery leaves

1. Melt the butter in a large pan and fry the onion gently without browning for about 5 minutes.
2. Add the carrots and celery, cover the pan and cook gently for a few minutes more until the butter is absorbed.
3. Stir in the cornflour then add the stock and tomato purée. Bring to the boil, half cover the pan and simmer for about 20 minutes until the vegetables are crisply tender. [F]
4. Meanwhile make the omelette. Beat the eggs with the salt and pepper. Melt the butter in a small frying pan, add the beaten eggs and fry until set and very pale brown on the underside. Turn the omelette over and brown the other side. Slide on to a plate and cut into 1 cm (½ inch) dice.
5. Taste the soup and season with pepper and a little salt if needed. Stir in the chopped parsley.
6. Serve in individual bowls garnished with a few pieces of the omelette and a celery leaf.

[F] Can be frozen in a plastic container for up to 6 weeks. Thaw overnight at room temperature and reheat gently.

VEGETABLE STOCK

Preparation time: 10 minutes
Cooking time: 2 hours
Makes about 1.75 litres (3 pints)

1 tablespoon vegetable oil
2 medium onions, about 350 g (12 oz), peeled and quartered
3 celery sticks, scrubbed, trimmed and cut into chunks
4 large carrots, about 450 g (1 lb), scrubbed and cut into chunks
1 teaspoon tomato purée
6 black peppercorns
1 teaspoon salt
2.25 litres (4 pints) water

Homemade stock makes all the difference to vegetarian recipes. It takes only minutes to prepare and can then be left to simmer away with no further attention. Keep the salt to a minimum and never add green leafy vegetables like cabbage as they spoil the background flavour.

1. Heat half the oil in a very large saucepan with a lid and fry the onions until quite dark brown. Remove and reserve, then brown the celery.
2. Put all the vegetables back into the pan and add the tomato purée, peppercorns, salt and water.
3. Bring to the boil, stirring at first, so that the colour from the bottom of the pan is mixed into the stock. Cover and simmer at the lowest possible heat for about 2 hours.
4. Strain the stock and leave to cool. [A] [F]

[A] The stock can be prepared up to 3 days in advance and stored in the refrigerator.
[F] The stock can be frozen for up to 1 month. Freeze in 600ml (1 pint) rigid containers, leaving headspace.

MUSHROOM AND HAZELNUT SOUP

Preparation time: 15 minutes
Cooking time: 20 minutes

25 g (1 oz) butter
350 g (12 oz) mushrooms, sliced
25 g (1 oz) ground hazelnuts
450 ml (¾ pint) Vegetable stock (see left)
450 ml (¾ pint) milk
¼ teaspoon grated nutmeg
salt
freshly ground black pepper
3 tablespoons single cream

Hazelnuts give this soup a distinctive flavour and thicken it too.
1. Melt the butter in a large pan, add the mushrooms and stir over a medium heat for 2-3 minutes until the juices run. Put the lid on the pan and simmer gently in the juices for 5 minutes. Take out 2 tablespoons of the mushrooms and reserve for garnishing later.
2. Stir in the hazelnuts, then add the stock, milk, nutmeg, salt and pepper. Cover and simmer gently for 10 minutes.
3. Blend the soup in a liquidizer or food processor until smooth. Return to the rinsed-out pan, stir in the cream and the reserved cooked mushrooms and gently reheat until piping hot but not boiling.
4. Check and adjust the seasoning if necessary. Serve immediately.

From the top: Light Vegetable Soup, Mushroom and Hazelnut Soup

11

VICHYSSOISE

Preparation time: 15 minutes
Cooking time: 50 minutes
Serves 6-8

450 g (1 lb) leeks, trimmed
450 g (1 lb) potatoes, peeled and sliced
1 medium onion, peeled and sliced
50 g (2 oz) butter or margarine
1.5 litres (2½ pints) Chicken stock
(see page 14)
freshly ground white pepper
150 ml (¼ pint) single cream
To garnish:
snipped chives or chopped parsley

1. Finely slice the white part of the leeks and about 5 cm (2 inches) of the green.
2. Sauté the leeks, potatoes and onion gently in the butter in a covered pan until soft.
3. Add the stock and simmer for 40-45 minutes until all the vegetables are soft, then liquidize in a blender until very smooth.
4. Chill thoroughly and adjust the seasoning. Just before serving, swirl in the cream and garnish with fresh chives or parsley.

MINESTRONE

Preparation time: 30 minutes, plus overnight soaking
Cooking time: 2½ hours
Serves 6

2 tablespoons olive oil
100 g (4 oz) bacon, diced
1 onion, peeled and chopped
1 garlic clove, peeled and chopped
225 g (8 oz) tomatoes, skinned and chopped
100 g (4 oz) dried borlotti or red kidney beans, soaked overnight
6 basil leaves, chopped
1 parsley sprig, chopped
2 litres (3½ pints) water
1 carrot, scraped and diced
1 celery stick, diced
275 g (10 oz) potatoes, peeled and diced
225 g (8 oz) courgettes, diced
225 g (8 oz) cabbage, shredded
100 g (4 oz) fresh peas, shelled, or frozen peas
200 g (7 oz) rice or small pasta shells
salt
freshly ground black pepper
50 g (2 oz) Parmesan cheese, grated

1. Heat the oil in a large saucepan, add the bacon, onion and garlic and sauté for a few minutes.
2. Add the tomatoes, beans, basil, parsley and water. Bring to the boil. Lower the heat, cover and simmer for about 1½ hours, stirring occasionally.
3. Add the carrot and celery and simmer for a further 30 minutes. Add the potatoes, courgettes, cabbage, peas and rice with salt and pepper to taste. Simmer for 20 minutes or until all the vegetables and beans are tender. Add pasta, if using, 10 minutes before the end of the cooking time.
4. Taste and adjust the seasoning. Stir in the Parmesan and serve.

BORSCHT

Preparation time: 25 minutes
Cooking time: 45 minutes
Serves 6-7

4 tablespoons vegetable oil
2 large onions, peeled and chopped
2 celery sticks, chopped
3 potatoes, about 350 g (12 oz), peeled and diced
1 large green pepper, cored, seeded and diced
1 × 225 g (8 oz) can tomatoes, roughly chopped
3 garlic cloves, peeled and crushed
3 large raw beetroot, about 450 g (1 lb), peeled and grated
1.25 litres (2¼ pints) Chicken stock (see page 14)
1 bay leaf
1 teaspoon dill seeds, crushed
2 sprigs parsley, finely chopped
salt
freshly ground black pepper
2 tablespoons wine vinegar
150 ml (¼ pint) soured cream or plain unsweetened yogurt

1. Heat the oil in a large saucepan, add the onions, celery, potatoes and green pepper and fry over a gentle heat for about 5 minutes, stirring occasionally, until the onion is soft.
2. Add the tomatoes, garlic, grated beetroot, stock and herbs. Bring to the boil, then lower the heat and simmer very gently for about 35 minutes, until the vegetables are tender. Taste and adjust the seasoning, add the wine vinegar and simmer for a further 5 minutes.
3. Remove the bay leaf and serve the soup, with soured cream or yogurt swirled over each bowl.

From the left: *Borscht, Vichyssoise, Minestrone*

CHINESE BEAN-SPROUT SOUP

Preparation time: 15 minutes
Cooking time: 30 minutes

1 litre (1¾ pints) Chicken stock
(see below)
1 medium onion, peeled and quartered
2 carrots, scraped and quartered
4 spring onions, thinly sliced
225 g (8 oz) fresh bean-sprouts
salt
freshly-ground black pepper
2 tablespoons soy sauce
2 tablespoons dry sherry
2 large radishes, sliced, to garnish

1. Put the stock in a pan with the onion and carrots, bring to the boil, cover and simmer for 20 minutes.
2. Strain the stock thoroughly and discard all the vegetables.
3. Return the stock to the pan, add the thinly sliced spring onions and bean-sprouts, and season with salt and pepper. Bring to the boil and simmer gently for 2-3 minutes.
4. Stir in the soy sauce and sherry, taste and adjust seasoning if necessary.
5. Serve the soup in individual dishes and garnish each one with radish slices.

CHICKEN STOCK

Preparation time: 10 minutes, plus cooling
Cooking time: 2-2½ hours
Makes about 1.75 litres (3 pints)

450 g (1 lb) chicken pieces
5 pints water
1 medium onion, peeled and quartered
1 carrot, scrubbed and cut into chunks
2 celery sticks, scrubbed and cut into chunks
1 bouquet garni (thyme, parsley, bay leaf)

1. Put all the ingredients in a large saucepan and bring slowly to the boil, skimming any foam off the surface.
2. Partially cover the pan and simmer gently for 2-2½ hours, until the liquid has been reduced by about one third.
3. Allow the stock to cool, then strain through a fine sieve. [A] [F]

[A] The stock may be kept in the refrigerator for up to one week.
[F] Freeze for up to six months.

From the left: Almond Soup, Chinese Bean-Sprout Soup, Gingered Pumpkin Soup

ALMOND SOUP

Preparation time: 15 minutes
Cooking time: 1 hour

1 litre (1¾ pints) Chicken stock
(see page 14)
2 celery sticks, chopped
1 small onion, peeled and quartered
1 bouquet garni
2 bay leaves
1 mace blade
salt
freshly ground white pepper
225 g (8 oz) blanched almonds, ground
100 ml (3½ fl oz) sweet sherry
120 ml (4 fl oz) plain unsweetened yogurt
(see note below)
40 g (1½ oz) flaked almonds, toasted, to
garnish

If you use homemade yogurt, it will need
to be stabilized before adding the soup,
otherwise it might separate. To do this, stir
in 1 teaspoon flour and heat gently in a
small pan, stirring constantly.
1. Put the stock into a pan, add the celery,
onion, bouquet garni, bay leaves and mace
and season with salt and pepper.
2. Bring slowly to the boil, uncovered, and
skim off any foam from the top. Cover the
pan and simmer for about 25 minutes.
3. Strain the stock, discarding the
flavourings, and return it to the pan.
4. Stir in the ground almonds, add the
sherry, cover and simmer for 20 minutes.
F
5. Stir in the yogurt and heat gently. Taste
and adjust seasoning if necessary.
6. Scatter the soup with the toasted
almonds. Serve hot.

F Freeze for up to 3 months. Thaw at room
temperature for 4-5 hours, then reheat and
continue from step 5.

GINGERED PUMPKIN SOUP

Preparation time: 15 minutes
Cooking time: 40 minutes
Serves 6

1 kg (2¼ lb) slice of pumpkin, peeled,
seeded and roughly chopped
1 piece fresh ginger, peeled
1 tablespoon sunflower oil
1 large onion, peeled and chopped
2 teaspoons ground ginger
1 teaspoon ground turmeric
2 large, ripe tomatoes, skinned and
chopped
2 teaspoons soft light brown sugar
¼ teaspoon grated nutmeg
strip thinly-pared orange rind
600 ml (1 pint) Chicken stock
(see page 14)
salt
freshly ground black pepper
300 ml (½ pint) plain unsweetened yogurt
(stabilized if homemade, see above)
To garnish:
2 tablespoons chopped parsley
6 tablespoons pumpkin seeds

1. Put the pumpkin into a pan with the
piece of ginger and cover it with water.
Bring to the boil, cover the pan and
simmer for 15 minutes, or until the
pumpkin is tender. Drain thoroughly and
remove the ginger.
2. Heat the oil in the pan and fry the onion
over moderate heat for 2 minutes. Stir in
the ground ginger and turmeric and cook
for 1 minute.
3. Add the pumpkin, tomatoes, sugar,
nutmeg, orange rind and stock and bring
to the boil. Cover and simmer for 10
minutes. Cool slightly. Discard the orange
rind. F
4. Liquidize the pumpkin mixture in a
blender, then return the purée to the pan.
Season with salt and pepper and stir in the
yogurt. Heat gently. Taste and adjust
seasoning if necessary.
5. Garnish the soup with the parsley and
pumpkin seeds.

F Freeze for up to 3 months. Thaw at room
temperature for 4-5 hours, then reheat and
continue from step 4.

CURRIED CAULIFLOWER SOUP

Preparation time: 15 minutes
Cooking time: 30 minutes

1 tablespoon sunflower oil
1 medium onion, peeled and sliced
2 teaspoons curry powder (or to taste)
1 small cauliflower, roughly chopped
900 ml (1½ pints) Chicken stock
(see page 14)
salt
freshly ground black pepper
4 tablespoons sunflower seeds, to garnish

1. Heat the oil in a large pan and fry the onion over moderate heat for 2 minutes. Stir in the curry powder and cook for 1 minute.
2. Add the cauliflower and stock, season with salt and pepper and bring to the boil. Cover the pan and simmer for 20 minutes.
3. Cool slightly, then liquidize the vegetables and stock in a blender. [F]
4. Return the purée to the pan. Taste and adjust the seasoning if necessary and reheat.
5. Garnish the soup with the sunflower seeds.

Variation: To add interesting texture to the soup, cut off a few very small cauliflower florets before blending and set them aside. Add them to the purée in the pan.

[F] Freeze for up to 3 months. Thaw at room temperature for 4-5 hours, then reheat and garnish with sunflower seeds.

SPINACH SOUP

Preparation time: 30 minutes
Cooking time: 20 minutes

750 g (1½ lb) fresh spinach, washed thoroughly and stalks removed
25 g (1 oz) butter
1 small onion, peeled and finely chopped
25 g (1 oz) plain flour
600 ml (1 pint) Vegetable stock
(see page 10)
about 300 ml (½ pint) milk
salt
freshly ground black pepper
freshly grated nutmeg
To garnish:
2 tablespoons plain unsweetened yogurt
(stabilized, if homemade; see page 15)
4 lemon slices (optional)

Illustrated on page 8

If fresh spinach is not available use a 275 g (10 oz) pack of frozen spinach instead. Spinach should be cooked for the shortest possible time to retain its colour and nutritional value, so for this soup it is cooked separately. No water is necessary.
1. Cook the spinach without water in a covered pan for 6-8 minutes, then turn into a bowl. (Heat frozen spinach just until thawed.)
2. Rinse out the pan and melt the butter in it. Add the chopped onion, fry gently without browning for 5 minutes then add the flour. Cook for 3 minutes, then pour in the stock. Stir well, bring to the boil and simmer for 3-4 minutes.
3. Cool slightly, then pour into a liquidizer or food processor, add the cooked spinach and blend until smooth.
4. Pour back into the pan and stir in sufficient milk to give a pouring consistency.
5. Add salt, pepper and nutmeg to taste.
[F] Reheat and serve, garnishing each bowl with yogurt and a slice of lemon, if liked.

[F] Can be frozen in a plastic container for up to 6 weeks. Thaw overnight at room temperature and reheat gently.

CELERIAC AND ORANGE SOUP

Preparation time: 20 minutes
Cooking time: 45 minutes
Serves 6

1 celeriac, about 350 g (12 oz), peeled and
roughly chopped
1 medium potato, peeled and roughly
chopped
2 medium carrots, scraped and sliced
1 litre (1¾ pints) Chicken stock
(see page 14)
thinly pared rind of ½ orange
1 teaspoon grated orange rind
1 tablespoon orange juice
salt
freshly ground black pepper
6 tablespoons plain unsweetened yogurt
(stabilized if homemade, see page 15)

1. Put the celeriac, potato and carrots into
a pan with the stock and bring to the boil.
Cover the pan and simmer for 30 minutes,
or until all the vegetables are soft.
2. Cut the orange rind into very thin
matchstick strips. Place them in a saucepan
with a little boiling water and boil for 10
minutes, then drain. Reserve for garnish.
3. Cool the vegetables and stock slightly,
then liquidize in a blender.
4. Return the purée to the pan, add the
grated orange rind and juice and season
with salt and pepper. Bring back to the boil
and simmer for 5 minutes. [F]
5. To serve, pour the soup into individual
dishes or bowls, swirl 1 tablespoon yogurt
on to each portion and garnish with strips
of orange rind.

[F] Freeze for up to 3 months. Thaw at room
temperature for 4-5 hours, then reheat and
continue from step 5.

Celeriac and Orange
Soup, Curried
Cauliflower Soup

French Onion Soup, Sweetcorn and Crab Soup

FRENCH ONION SOUP

Preparation time: 15 minutes
Cooking time: 50 minutes-1 hour
Serves 5

50 g (2 oz) butter
750 g (1½ lb) onions, peeled and thinly sliced
2 teaspoons sugar
2 teaspoons plain flour
1 litre (2¾ pints) beef stock
salt
freshly ground black pepper
½ French loaf, sliced
50 g (2 oz) Gruyère cheese, grated

1. Melt the butter in a pan, add the onions and sugar. Lower the heat and cook the onions slowly for 20-30 minutes, until they are an even chestnut brown. Take care to cook them slowly, so that they brown evenly and to a good colour without burning.
2. Add the flour and cook for about 5 minutes, stirring well. Add the stock, salt and pepper. Bring to the boil and simmer for 15-20 minutes.
3. Meanwhile, place the slices of French bread under a preheated grill and toast on one side. Cover the other side with the grated cheese and toast until golden brown.
4. Taste and adjust the seasoning, then pour the soup into a hot tureen. Place a piece of toast in each serving dish and pour the soup over.

SWEETCORN AND CRAB SOUP

Preparation time: 15 minutes
Cooking time: about 5 minutes

1 teaspoon finely chopped ginger root
100 g (4 oz) crab meat
2 teaspoons sherry
1 egg white
3 teaspoons cornflour
2 tablespoons cold water
600 ml (1 pint) Chicken stock (p 14)
1 teaspoon salt
100 g (4 oz) sweetcorn
1 spring onion, finely chopped, to garnish

1. Mix the ginger root with the crab and sherry.
2. Beat the egg white and mix the cornflour with the water to a smooth paste.
3. Bring the stock to a rolling boil, then add the salt, sweetcorn and crab meat. When it starts to boil again, add the cornflour and water mixture, stirring constantly.
4. Add the egg white, stirring.
5. Garnish the soup with finely chopped spring onion and serve hot.

CARROT AND LENTIL SOUP

Preparation time: 20 minutes
Cooking time: 45 minutes

25 g (1 oz) butter
1 medium onion, peeled and chopped
1 clove garlic, peeled and crushed
(optional)
2 carrots, about 100 g (4 oz), scrubbed and chopped
2 sticks celery, trimmed, scrubbed and chopped
150 g (5 oz) red lentils, washed and drained
1 litre (1¾ pints) Vegetable stock
(see page 10)
salt
freshly ground black pepper
2 teaspoons lemon juice
about 150 ml (5 fl oz) milk
2 tablespoons chopped fresh parsley
Croûtons:
oil, for shallow frying
4 slices wholemeal bread, crusts removed and cut into 1 cm (½ inch) cubes

Illustrated on page 8

Few things are as comforting as a bowl of hot homemade soup. This one freezes well so it is a good one to make in advance ready to thaw and reheat. Served with hot garlic or herb bread and fresh fruit it makes a nourishing meal.
1. Melt the butter in a large pan and fry the onion and garlic for 5 minutes until soft but not brown.
2. Add the carrots, celery and lentils and stir around in the butter for a few minutes. Pour in the stock, half cover the pan and simmer very gently for about 40 minutes, stirring occasionally.
3. Pour the soup into a liquidizer or food processor and blend until smooth. Pour back into the saucepan and season with salt and pepper. Add the lemon juice and thin the soup with milk to the consistency you prefer.
4. Taste and adjust the seasoning. [F] Stir in the parsley.
5. Keep the soup just simmering while you make the croûtons. Heat a little oil in a frying pan and fry the bread cubes in 2 batches until golden brown. Drain on kitchen paper.
6. Serve the soup piping hot in individual bowls, sprinkling with the croûtons at the last moment.

[F] Can be frozen in a plastic container for up to 6 weeks. Thaw overnight at room temperature and reheat gently, then stir in the parsley.

PÂTÉS & TERRINES

Coarsely textured, fine and silky-smooth, colourfully layered, light and mousse-like: there is a pâté, terrine or potted savoury starter in almost every guise.

When a starter precedes a hearty main course and rich dessert opt for a light smooth-textured pâté like Liver and Mushroom Pâté and serve with crisp biscuits or a colourful assembly of salad greenery. Leave more robust and richer offerings like Pâté de Campagne for when the starter is the appetite-satisfying anchor of the meal.

Most pâtés and terrines are perfect served with chunky slices of bread but ring the changes occasionally by serving them with water biscuits, wafer-thin curls of almost transparent Melba toast, discs of bought or home-made wholewheat crackers, pull-apart slices of aromatic garlic bread, crisp triangles of warm toast or on a simple bed of complementary salad.

Generally made well ahead, these are the ideal starters to serve when you are planning an elaborate main course like pan-fried Veal Schnitzels, Chicken Cordon Bleu or grilled or fried steak favourites like Steak Diane and Tournedos Rossini. Round off the meal with a creamy ice cream, frozen sorbet, parfait or sundae made in advance and stored in the freezer so that you can take a relaxing back seat towards the end of the meal. If the chosen pâté or terrine starter is rich, then choose a light refreshing fruity sorbet for dessert; but when the starter is easy on the calories you may opt for rich creamy ice creams laden with fruits and nuts and served with indulgent crisp biscuits and wafers to finish the meal.

Almost all pâtés and terrines can be made up to 2 days in advance and stored in the refrigerator. To prevent them from drying out cover with stretch-wrap (removed before serving) or a thin layer of clarified butter. Top this golden buttery layer with arrangements of citrus slices or quarters, whole sprigs or bundles of herbs, sprinklings of whole or chopped nuts or a judicious addition of liquor-soaked fruit like cherries for the ultimate finishing touch. Pâtés and terrines may be presented whole in an attractive dish or sliced or scooped on to individual plates, cleverly and colourfully garnished in an infinite variety of styles.

Crab and Shrimp Terrine (page 33), Nouvelle Chicken Liver Pâté (page 33)

CREAMED SMOKED MACKEREL POTS

Preparation time: 10 minutes, plus chilling

1 medium smoked mackerel, about 225 g
(8 oz), skinned, boned and finely flaked
65 g (2½ oz) butter, melted
50 g (2 oz) full fat soft cheese
1 teaspoon lemon juice
1 tablespoon chopped fresh parsley
½-1 teaspoon creamed horseradish
(optional)
freshly ground black pepper
To garnish:
lemon slices
parsley sprigs

This unusual pâté is quick and easy to make and delicious served with bread or wholewheat crackers.
1. Place the mackerel in a bowl. Add 25 g (1 oz) of the melted butter with the cheese and stir well to mix.
2. Stir in the lemon juice, parsley, creamed horseradish, if using, and pepper to taste. Mix thoroughly until well combined.
3. Divide the mixture evenly between 4 small individual ramekins or serving pots and smooth the surfaces.
4. Pour the remaining melted butter over each ramekin and chill in the refrigerator for at least 2 hours before serving, garnished with lemon slices and parsley sprigs.

LIVER AND MUSHROOM PÂTÉ

Preparation time: 15 minutes, plus chilling
Cooking time: 20 minutes
Serves 4-5

65 g (2½ oz) butter
1 garlic clove, peeled and chopped
1 medium onion, peeled and thinly sliced
4 rashers streaky bacon, rinded and diced
100 g (4 oz) button mushrooms, sliced
225 g (8 oz) chicken livers, trimmed
150 ml (¼ pint) Chicken stock (see page 14)
2 hard-boiled eggs, shelled and chopped
1½ tablespoons single cream
salt
freshly ground black pepper
To garnish:
4 bay leaves
black peppercorns

1. Melt 40 g (1½ oz) of the butter in a frying pan. Add the garlic, onion and bacon and fry over a moderate heat for 5 minutes.
2. Stir in the mushrooms and chicken livers and fry for a further 5 minutes, stirring frequently.
3. Add the stock and bring to the boil. Cover with a lid or foil and cook over a gentle heat for 10 minutes.
4. Strain the mixture and process in a food processor or blender for about 30 seconds, until smooth. Add the hard-boiled eggs, cream and salt and pepper to taste and blend again until smooth and thoroughly combined. Add a little stock to blend if necessary.
5. Turn the mixture into a 300 ml (½ pint) serving dish and smooth the surface. $\boxed{A}$ $\boxed{F}$ Melt the remaining butter and pour over the top of the pâté. Garnish with the bay leaves and peppercorns, then chill in the refrigerator for at least 4 hours before serving.

$\boxed{A}$ Can be prepared 2 days in advance, covered with cling film and kept chilled.
$\boxed{F}$ Freeze for up to 1 month. Thaw overnight in the refrigerator before covering with melted butter and garnishing with bay leaves and peppercorns.
$\boxed{M}$ Or microwave on Defrost for 4-6 minutes, then stand for 1 hour before covering with melted butter.

FARMHOUSE TERRINE

*Preparation time: 20 minutes, plus setting and
chilling overnight
Cooking time: 2½ hours
Oven: 160°C, 325°F, Gas Mark 3*
Serves 8-10

10 rashers streaky bacon, rinded and
boned
450 g (1 lb) pig's liver, coarsely minced
450 g (1 lb) lean pork, coarsely minced
1 medium onion, peeled and finely
chopped
2 garlic cloves, peeled and crushed
½ teaspoon dried thyme or mixed herbs
1 tablespoon dry sherry
50 g (2 oz) fresh wholemeal breadcrumbs
½ teaspoon salt
freshly ground black pepper

1. Place the bacon rashers on a board and
flatten them with the flat side of a knife
until double their original length.
2. Line a 1 kg (2 lb) loaf tin with bacon,
slightly overlapping along the length of the
tin, allowing the ends to overlap the rim of
the tin on each of the longer sides.
3. Mix the remaining ingredients well
together and turn into the bacon-lined tin,
smoothing the surface. Fold the
overlapping ends of the bacon rashers over
the mixture.
4. Cover the tin tightly with foil and place
in a roasting tin. Pour in cold water to
come halfway up the sides of the loaf tin.
Cook in a preheated oven for 2½ hours.
5. Remove the foil and cover with fresh
foil, weight down and leave to cool for 3
hours. Then chill overnight, in the
refrigerator, still weighted down. F

F Freeze for up to 1 month. Thaw
overnight in the refrigerator.
M Or microwave on Defrost for 12-15
minutes, then stand for 2-3 hours.

*Clockwise from the left:
Liver and Mushroom
Pâté, Farmhouse Terrine,
Creamed Smoked
Mackerel Pots*

PÂTÉ DE CAMPAGNE

*Preparation time: 30 minutes, plus cooling
and chilling
Cooking time: 2½ hours
Oven: 160°C, 325°F, Gas Mark 3*
Serves 8-10

oil, for brushing
8 streaky bacon rashers, rinds removed
450 g (1 lb) pig's liver
450 g (1 lb) chicken livers
225 g (8 oz) pork back fat or fatty belly pork
175 g (6 oz) fresh white breadcrumbs
2 eggs, beaten
2 garlic cloves, peeled and crushed with ½
teaspoon salt
75 ml (3 fl oz) red wine
2 tablespoons brandy (optional)
2 teaspoons freshly chopped thyme or 1
teaspoon dried thyme
40-50 g (1½-2 oz) pistachio nuts, coarsely
chopped
freshly ground black pepper

1. Brush the inside of a 1 kg (2 lb) loaf tin or a 1.2 litre (2 pint) earthenware dish with oil. Stretch the bacon rashers with the blade of a knife, then use to line the base and sides of the tin or dish. Set aside.
2. Mince together the pig's liver, chicken livers and pork, then place in a bowl. Add the remaining ingredients with pepper to taste, and stir well.
3. Spoon into the prepared tin and level the surface. Cover with foil, then stand the tin in a bain-marie (roasting tin half filled with hot water). Bake in a preheated oven for 2½ hours until the pâté and the juices are just faintly pink.
4. Remove from the oven and pour off the excess fat from the tin, leave until cool, then place heavy weights on top of the foil to press the pâté into a firm shape for slicing. When completely cold, place in the refrigerator and chill overnight.
5. Run knife round edge of pâté to release the bacon from the tin, then turn pâté out on to a plate. Serve cut into thick slices.

DUCK TERRINE

*Preparation time: 1-1¼ hours, plus chilling
Cooking time: 1½ hours
Oven: 160°C, 325°F, Gas Mark 3*
Serves 6-8

1 × 2-2.25 kg (4½-5 lb) oven-ready duck
2 tablespoons brandy
225 g (8 oz) chicken livers
225 g (8 oz) pork sausagemeat
50 g (2 oz) fresh white breadcrumbs
finely grated rind and juice of 1 orange
6 juniper berries, crushed
¼ teaspoon ground allspice
salt
freshly ground black pepper
1 egg, beaten, to bind
1 orange, thinly sliced

1. Bone the duck, removing as much meat as possible from the bones. Cut 75-100 g (3-4 oz) breast meat into slivers, place in a dish and pour over the brandy.
2. Mince the remaining duck meat with the liver from the duck and the chicken livers. Place in a bowl with the sausagemeat, mix well, add the breadcrumbs, orange rind and juice, juniper, allspice, and salt and pepper and mix again. Drain the brandy from the slivers of duck and stir the brandy into the mixture. Bind with egg.
3. Brush a 900 ml (1½ pint) terrine or mould lightly with oil. Arrange the orange slices in the base, then spoon in half the minced mixture, packing it down well. Arrange the drained slivers of breast evenly over the top, spoon in the remaining minced mixture and press down firmly.
4. Cover the mould with lightly oiled foil, then stand it in a bain-marie (roasting tin half filled with hot water). Cook in a preheated oven for 1½ hours or until the juices run faintly pink and the terrine has shrunk away from the sides of the mould.
5. Remove from the bain-marie and pour off the excess fat and juices in the bottom of the mould. Leave until cold, then chill overnight until firm.
6. Serve chilled, cut into thick slices.

*Top: Pâté de
Campagne; **bottom:**
Duck Terrine*

SMOKED CHICKEN PÂTÉ

Preparation time: 10 minutes, plus chilling
Serves 6

225 g (8 oz) smoked chicken, skinned and
chopped
rind of ½ lemon
3 tablespoons lemon juice
1 tablespoon snipped chives
150 ml (¼ pint) soured cream
50 g (2 oz) butter
salt
freshly ground black pepper
To garnish:
lemon quarters or twists
chive bundles

1. Place all the ingredients in a blender or
food processor. Purée until smooth and
creamy.
2. Spoon into 1 large or 6 small serving
dishes, cover with cling film and chill to
set. [A]
3. Garnish with lemon and chive bundles,
and serve with crackers.

[A] The pâté can be made up to 3 days in
advance, if covered and chilled.

Illustrated on page 29

TERRINE DE RIS DE VEAU

*Preparation time: 20-30 minutes, plus
soaking, marinating and cooling
Cooking time: 1 hour 40 minutes
Oven: 190°C, 375°F, Gas Mark 5*
Serves 8-12

100 g (4 oz) sweetbreads
4 tablespoons white wine
2 tablespoons brandy
75 g (3 oz) butter
1 onion, peeled and finely chopped
1 garlic clove, peeled and crushed
350 g (12 oz) lean minced pork
350 g (12 oz) minced veal
1 egg, beaten
salt
freshly ground black pepper
pinch of nutmeg
225 g (8 oz) thinly sliced streaky bacon
rashers, rinded

1. Soak the sweetbreads in cold water for
1-2 hours.
2. Drain the sweetbreads, place in a pan of
boiling salted water and blanch for 2-3
minutes. Drain again and place in cold
water, then remove the membranes.
3. Slice the sweetbreads, put into a bowl
with the wine and brandy, and leave to
marinate for 1-2 hours.
4. Melt 25 g (1 oz) of the butter, add the
onion and cook until soft but not coloured.
5. Mix the garlic with the onion, and place
in a bowl with the minced pork, veal and
egg. Add salt, pepper, nutmeg and the
sweetbread marinating liquor. Mix well.
6. Line a 1 kg (2 lb) terrine with bacon.
Place a layer of the pork mixture in the
bottom. Put the sweetbreads on top and
cover with the remainder of the pork
mixture. Cover the top with bacon.
7. Put the terrine in a bain-marie or
roasting tin of hot water. Cook in a
preheated oven for about 1½ hours. The
terrine is cooked when it has shrunk
slightly from the sides of the dish and the
surrounding fat and juices are clear, not
pink.
8. When cooked, cool for 30 minutes, then
cover with greaseproof paper or foil and
place a weight on top. (A 1 kg (2 lb) bag of
sugar is ideal.) Leave until cold and set.
9. Melt the remaining butter in a pan and
pour over the top of the terrine. [F]

[F] It will keep unopened for 5-7 days in a
refrigerator, or 1 month in the freezer.
Thaw overnight in the refrigerator.

Terrine de Ris de Veau

ALL SEASONS PORK PÂTÉ

*Preparation time: 30 minutes, plus cooling
and chilling
Cooking time: 2-2¼ hours
Oven: 180°C, 350°F, Gas Mark 4*
Serves 8

225 g (8 oz) streaky bacon rashers, rinded
450 g (1 lb) pork liver, minced
350 g (12 oz) lean pork (eg fillet or leg),
minced
225 g (8 oz) sausage meat
2 egg yolks
150 ml (¼ pint) double cream
3 tablespoons mild burger mustard
1 small onion, peeled and finely chopped
1 teaspoon dried sage
1 teaspoon dried marjoram
salt
freshly ground black pepper

1. Stretch the bacon with the back of a knife and arrange crosswise to line the base and sides of a 1 kg (2 lb) loaf tin.
2. Mix the liver with the lean pork, sausage meat, egg yolks, cream, mustard, onion, sage, marjoram and salt and pepper to taste.
3. Spoon into the prepared tin and level the surface. Cover with a piece of buttered foil. Place in a bain-marie or roasting tin half-full of water. Cook in a preheated moderate oven for 2-2¼ hours.
4. Allow to cool slightly. Cover with a double thickness of foil, place a weight on top and leave to go cold. Chill the weighted pâté for at least 24 hours. [A]
5. Serve sliced with radishes, pickled onions or gherkins and crusty bread.

[A] The pâté can be made up to 3 days in advance, if covered and chilled.

WHISKY TERRINE

*Preparation time: 10 minutes, plus chilling
Cooking time: 25-30 minutes*
Serves 6

100 g (4 oz) butter
1 large onion, peeled and chopped
1 garlic clove, peeled and crushed
100 g (4 oz) streaky bacon, rinded and
chopped
225 g (8 oz) chicken livers
100 g (4 oz) button mushrooms, wiped
150 ml (¼ pint) whisky
finely grated rind of 1 lemon
2 tablespoons lemon juice
salt
freshly ground black pepper
1½ tablespoons chopped fresh parsley
2½ tablespoons fresh white breadcrumbs
2 small bay leaves
3 allspice berries

1. Melt the butter in a large pan. Add the onion and garlic and cook over a gentle heat for 10 minutes. Add the bacon, chicken livers and mushrooms and cook gently for 5 minutes.
2. Add the whisky, lemon rind, lemon juice and salt and pepper. Cover and simmer gently for 10-15 minutes.
3. Purée in a blender or food processor until smooth. Add the parsley and breadcrumbs and blend again to mix.
4. Spoon into a serving dish and level the surface. Press the bay leaves and allspice berries into the top. Cover with cling film and chill to set. [A]

[A] The terrine can be made up to 4 days in advance, if covered and chilled.

From the top: All Seasons Pork Pâté, Whisky Terrine, Smoked Chicken Pâté (page 27)

From the left: Vegetable Terrine, Potted Pork

POTTED PORK

Preparation time: 15 minutes, plus cooling and chilling
Cooking time: 2-2½ hours
Serves 8

1 kg (2 lb) belly of pork
2 garlic cloves, peeled and crushed
4 onions, peeled and finely chopped
2 teaspoons ground nutmeg
2 teaspoons dried thyme
1 teaspoon mild Madras curry powder
300 ml (½ pint) well-flavoured stock
4 bay leaves
salt
freshly ground black pepper
4-6 tablespoons melted clarified butter
6 whole black peppercorns

1. Remove the skin and bones from the pork and cut into cubes.
2. Place in a heavy-based pan with the garlic, onions, nutmeg, thyme, curry powder, stock, 2 of the bay leaves and salt and pepper to taste. Bring to the boil, lower the heat, then cover and simmer for 2-2½ hours, until the meat is very tender.
3. Drain the meat mixture, remove the bay leaves and chop in a blender or food processor until almost smooth. Alternatively, pound the mixture in a pestle and mortar or in a bowl with the end of a rolling pin.
4. Taste and adjust the seasoning if necessary and pack into a terrine. Cool, then chill lightly until almost set.
5. Cover the mixture with a layer of clarified butter. Top with the remaining bay leaves and peppercorns and chill to set. **A**
6. Serve with toast, crusty bread or Melba toast.

A The terrine can be made up to 4 days in advance, if covered and kept chilled.

VEGETABLE TERRINE

Preparation time: 1 hour
Cooking time: about 1¾ hours
Oven: 160°C, 325°F, Gas Mark 3
Serves 6

2 tablespoons olive oil
1 onion, peeled and thinly sliced
350 g (12 oz) courgettes, sliced
350 g (12 oz) frozen chopped spinach,
thawed
salt
freshly ground black pepper
½ teaspoon freshly grated nutmeg
225 g (8 oz) curd cheese
50 g (2 oz) fresh white breadcrumbs
2 teaspoons freshly chopped basil or 1
teaspoon dried basil
2 teaspoons freshly chopped marjoram or 1
teaspoon dried marjoram (optional)
1 egg, beaten
melted butter for greasing tin

1. Heat the oil in a frying pan, add the onion and courgettes and fry gently until soft and lightly coloured. Remove from the pan with a slotted spoon, then place in a single layer on paper towels. Cover with more paper towels and press to remove excess oil.
2. Put the spinach in a heavy-based pan and heat gently until thoroughly dry, stirring frequently. Remove from the heat and stir in generous amounts of salt, pepper and the nutmeg.
3. Work the courgettes and onions into a purée in an electric blender or vegetable mill, then place in a heavy-based pan and dry out over gentle heat as with the spinach. Transfer to a bowl, then beat in the curd cheese, breadcrumbs, basil, marjoram (if using), and salt and pepper to taste. Bind with the beaten egg.
4. Brush the inside of a 450 g (1 lb) loaf tin liberally with butter, line the base with greaseproof paper, then brush with more butter. Put half the courgette mixture in the bottom of the tin, pressing it down firmly and levelling the surface. Spread the spinach in an even layer over the top, then press in the remaining courgette mixture.
5. Cover the tin with buttered foil, then stand it in a bain-marie (roasting tin half filled with hot water) and bake in a preheated oven for 1¼ hours or until the mixture feels firm and set when a knife is inserted in the centre.
6. Remove from the bain-marie, leave the terrine in the tin until completely cold, then chill in the refrigerator overnight until firm.
7. Loosen the sides of the terrine from the tin with a knife, then carefully turn out on to a serving plate and peel off the greaseproof paper. Serve chilled, cut into thick slices.

Fresh Salmon Pâté

FRESH SALMON PÂTÉ

Preparation time: 40 minutes, plus cooling
Cooking time: 40 minutes
Serves 12

750 g (1½ lb) fresh salmon or sea-trout
1 small onion, peeled and sliced
1 carrot, peeled and sliced
2 bay leaves
150 ml (¼ pint) white wine
175 g (6 oz) unsalted butter, creamed
Sauce:
75 g (3 oz) butter
75 g (3 oz) plain flour
600 ml (1 pint) milk
2 teaspoons lemon juice
salt
freshly ground black pepper
To garnish:
½ cucumber, cut into thin rings
1 hard-boiled egg, yolk sieved, white chopped
1 tablespoon chopped fresh parsley

If making this pâté in advance, do not garnish until ready to serve.
1. Place the salmon in a large saucepan and add the onion, carrot, bay leaves and wine. Add just enough water to cover, then bring the fish slowly to the boil. Simmer gently for 15-20 minutes, then remove from the heat and allow the fish to cool in the liquid.
2. Meanwhile make up the sauce base. Melt the butter in a saucepan, remove from the heat and stir in the flour. Cook the roux for 2-3 minutes, then gradually add the milk, beating well between each addition until really smooth. Simmer gently for 3-4 minutes, add the lemon juice, salt and pepper and allow to cool.
3. Skin and flake the cooked salmon, and pass it through a food processor or pound it with a pestle and mortar.
4. When all the ingredients are cool, blend together the fish, sauce and creamed butter. Check the seasoning and place the pâté in a dish. Cover with clingfilm until ready to garnish.
5. Arrange the cucumber round the outside, then the chopped egg white and finish with the egg yolk and parsley.

NOUVELLE CHICKEN LIVER PÂTÉ

Preparation time: 10 minutes
· Cooking time: about 40 minutes
Oven: 180°C, 350°F, Gas Mark 4

225 g (8 oz) chicken livers, trimmed
1 onion, peeled and chopped
1 garlic clove, peeled
50 g (2 oz) wholemeal bread
3 tablespoons skimmed milk
1 egg
50 g (2 oz) polyunsaturated margarine
2 teaspoons chopped mixed herbs
2 tablespoons Greek yogurt
salt
freshly ground black pepper
To garnish:
lemon wedges
sprigs fresh parsley

1. Place all the ingredients in a blender or food processor and purée until smooth. Divide equally between four small ovenproof dishes or ramekins. Cover with greased foil.
2. Place in a roasting pan with sufficient hot water to come halfway up the sides of the dishes. Cook in a preheated oven for about 40 minutes or until just set. Remove from the pan and leave until cool then chill. [A]
3. Serve lightly chilled, garnished with lemon wedges and parsley sprigs. Serve with toast or salad.

[A] The pâté may be made up to 2 days in advance, covered and kept chilled.

Illustrated on page 20

CRAB AND SHRIMP TERRINE

Preparation time: 20 minutes, plus chilling and setting
Serves: 4-6

225 g (8 oz) white crabmeat, flaked
300 ml (½ pint) lemon mayonnaise
150 ml (¼ pint) natural set yogurt
150 ml (¼ pint) soured cream
1 tablespoon chopped parsley or watercress
salt
freshly ground black pepper
225 g (8 oz) peeled shrimps, finely chopped
1 × 85 g (3 oz) packet soft cheese
1 teaspoon anchovy essence
1 teaspoon tomato purée
5 teaspoons powdered gelatine
100 ml (4 fl oz) boiling water
3 tablespoons lemon juice
2 tablespoons cold water
1 lemon, sliced
75 g (3 oz) peeled shrimps
curly endive to garnish (if liked)

If commercially-prepared lemon mayonnaise is not available, make it for this recipe by adding 1 tablespoon of fresh lemon juice to ½ pint of basic mayonnaise.
1. Mix the crabmeat with half of the mayonnaise, half of the yogurt, half of the soured cream, the parsley or watercress and salt and pepper to taste, blending well.
2. Mix the chopped shrimps with the remaining mayonnaise, yogurt, soured cream, soft cheese, anchovy essence, tomato purée and salt and pepper to taste.
3. Dissolve all but 1 teaspoon of the gelatine in the boiling water and stir half into the crab mixture and half into the shrimp mixture, blending well.
4. Spoon half of the shrimp mixture into a 1.2 litre (2 pint) terrine or dish and chill to set. Cover with half of the crab mixture and chill to set. Repeat the layers again, chilling and setting between each layer.
5. Place the remaining gelatine and lemon juice in a small bowl. Stand in a pan of hot water and heat until clear and dissolved. Add the cold water, blending well. Arrange lemon slices and whole peeled shrimps decoratively on the surface of the terrine and spoon over the lemon jelly to coat. Chill to set.
6. Serve chilled, garnished with endive.
Illustrated on page 20

SAVOURY STARTERS

Tender poached eggs in crisp pastry cases; colourful vegetables dipped in a creamy sauce; marinated meat on skewers; light-as-air mousses all feature here.

Most of these starters can be made in advance, providing ideal dishes to accompany classic main courses that demand last-minute attention like a fresh dover sole grilled with a sprinkling of lemon juice and dot of butter or sautéed calves' liver with chopped fresh sage.

Others, like Goat's Cheese and Avocado Special and Curried Egg Mayonnaise, have that wonderful virtue of simplicity and can be made and assembled in minutes so you can go all out for an exotic main course like roasted pigeons or quail with grape garnish; Veal Blanquette surrounded with crisp croûtons and bacon rolls; or fluffy fish quenelles with creamy herb-scented sauce. All are best served with simple but traditional desserts like pears poached in wine, Crème Caramel or, when the main dish is featherlight, a pastry, Jam Roly Poly, Spotted Dick or Spiced Bread Pudding.

Many of the recipes in this section have been inspired by the clever use and addition of cheese in all its guises. Others use light and flaky pastry as their foundation, showing off the skills of the competent pastrycook. Some assume no skills at all, like Greek Lamb and Cinnamon Skewers, so are perfect for the novice or beginner. Most have been created to make the best use of seasonal produce: Goat's Cheese and Avocado Special, for instance, relies heavily upon the summer bounty of ripe and mild avocado pears and Herb Quiche uses the best of spring vegetables and midsummer herbs. Mushrooms in Pastry Cases are best made with mellow autumn woodland or field mushrooms freshly bought or pickled; and Egg and Watercress Mousses use watercress at its best from early spring to mid-autumn. The versatile cook will, of course, find a few canny substitutes at different times of the year to give a variation on flavour.

*Clockwise from the left:
Curried Egg Mayonnaise
(page 38), Greek Lamb
and Cinnamon Skewers
(page 37), Cheese and
Tuna Oven-Baked
Muffins (page 44)*

From the top: Crispy Vegetables with Dolcelatte Dip, Goat's Cheese and Avocado Special

GOAT'S CHEESE AND AVOCADO SPECIAL

Preparation time: 20 minutes

175 g (6 oz) goat's cheese, rind removed
3 tablespoons snipped chives
2 tablespoons chopped fresh parsley
2 ripe avocados
1 tablespoon lemon juice
2 large grapefruit
4 tablespoons salad oil
1 tablespoon wine vinegar
salt
freshly ground black pepper

1. Cut the goat's cheese into bite-size pieces. Mix 2 tablespoons of the chives with the parsley. Roll the cheese in the herbs to coat lightly and divide equally between 4 individual serving dishes.
2. Peel, halve, stone and slice the avocado and toss in the lemon juice. Peel and segment the grapefruit, removing any pith and collecting any juice in a small bowl. Arrange the segments with the avocado slices on the serving plates.
3. Beat the oil with the vinegar, grapefruit juice, remaining chives and salt and pepper to taste. Spoon over the avocado and grapefruit. Serve as soon as possible.

GREEK LAMB AND CINNAMON SKEWERS

*Preparation time: 10 minutes, plus chilling
Cooking time: 7-8 minutes*

125 g (4 oz) Greek yogurt
2 tablespoons olive oil
2 tablespoons chopped fresh mint
1 garlic clove, peeled and crushed
2 tablespoons creamed honey
¼ teaspoon ground cinnamon
salt
freshly ground black pepper
450 g (1 lb) lamb neck fillet, trimmed and
cut into small cubes
8 bay leaves
lemon wedges to garnish

1. Mix the yogurt with the oil, mint, garlic, honey, cinnamon and salt and pepper to taste, blending well. Add the lamb and stir to coat. Cover and chill for 4 hours.
2. Drain the lamb from the marinade with a slotted spoon and thread on to four small skewers with the bay leaves.
3. Cook under a preheated hot grill or over medium coals on a barbecue for 7-8 minutes, basting frequently with the marinade, until cooked.
4. Serve hot garnished with lemon wedges and with any remaining marinade drizzled over.

Illustrated on page 34

CRISPY VEGETABLES WITH DOLCELATTE DIP

Preparation time: 20-25 minutes

Dip:
150 g (5 oz) Dolcelatte cheese, rind removed
200 ml (7 fl oz) soured cream
1 tablespoon French mustard
1 tablespoon capers, finely chopped
snipped chives
Vegetables:
4 large carrots, peeled and cut into thin strips
1 bunch spring onions, trimmed
1 small cauliflower, broken into small florets
4 celery sticks, scrubbed and cut into short lengths
1 head fennel, quartered and brushed with lemon juice
8 small cherry tomatoes, halved

1. Place the Dolcelatte, soured cream and mustard in a blender and purée until smooth. Alternatively, beat the cheese with a wooden spoon until creamy. Add cream and mustard.
2. Fold in the capers and spoon into a serving bowl. Sprinkle with snipped chives, cover and chill until required. [A]
3. Serve the dip surrounded by the vegetables attractively arranged.

[A] The dip can be made up to 2 days in advance, if covered and chilled.

CURRIED EGG MAYONNAISE

Preparation time: 10-15 minutes

150 ml (5 fl oz) mayonnaise
1 × 225 g (8 oz) can curried beans with sultanas
grated rind of ½ lemon
1½ tablespoons lemon juice
75 g (3 oz) cooked chicken, cut into thin strips
salt
freshly ground black pepper
½ crisp lettuce, shredded
4 hard-boiled eggs, shelled
To garnish:
paprika
sprigs of watercress (optional)

1. Mix the mayonnaise with the curried beans, lemon rind, lemon juice, chicken and salt and pepper to taste.
2. Place the lettuce on a serving dish and spoon over half the curried bean and chicken mixture. Top with the eggs, left whole or halved as preferred. Spoon the remaining curried bean mixture over and around the eggs.
3. Dust the eggs with a little paprika and garnish with watercress, if liked.

Illustrated on page 34

NESTING EGGS

Preparation time: about 40 minutes
Cooking time: about 25 minutes
Oven: 190°C, 375°F, Gas Mark 5

100 g (4 oz) Basic shortcrust pastry (see page 43)
100 g (4 oz) asparagus spears, cooked and chopped
salt
freshly ground black pepper
4 eggs
25 g (1 oz) butter
25 g (1 oz) plain flour
300 ml (½ pint) milk
50 g (2 oz) mature Cheddar cheese, grated
4 teaspoons grated Parmesan cheese
chopped fresh parsley, to garnish

1. Roll out the pastry on a lightly floured surface and cut out rounds large enough to line 4 large individual tartlet tins. Prick the bases and sides of the pastry thoroughly with a fork. Line with greaseproof paper and fill with baking beans, dried peas or lentils.
2. Bake in a preheated moderately hot oven for 15 minutes until golden brown and cooked through. Remove the greaseproof paper, beans, peas or lentils. Remove the tartlets from their tins.
3. Fill each tartlet shell with an equal quantity of the asparagus and add salt and pepper to taste.
4. Meanwhile, poach the eggs in simmering water for 3 minutes. Remove with a slotted spoon, drain well and trim. Gently place each egg in a tartlet.
5. Melt the butter in a pan. Add the flour and cook for 1 minute. Gradually add the milk and bring to the boil, stirring constantly. Cook for 2-3 minutes, remove from the heat and stir in the Cheddar cheese until melted.
6. Place each tartlet in an individual gratin dish and spoon over the sauce. Sprinkle with the Parmesan cheese and cook under a preheated hot grill for about 3 minutes until golden. Garnish with parsley and serve at once.

MUSTARD CHEESE TRUFFLES

Preparation time: 10-15 minutes, plus chilling
Makes about 24

225 g (8 oz) full fat soft cheese
100 g (4 oz) blue cheese
2 teaspoons Dijon mustard
freshly ground black pepper
4-5 slices pumpernickel bread or 8-10
cheese crackers, finely crumbed

1. Purée the cheeses, mustard and pepper in a blender or beat together with a wooden spoon until smooth and blended. [A]
2. Using a teaspoon, scoop walnut-sized pieces of the mixture and shape each into a ball. Roll in the pumpernickel or cracker crumbs to coat completely. Chill in the refrigerator until ready to serve.
3. Serve in a cucumber chain ring, if wished.

[A] The truffle mixture can be made up to 1 week in advance, if covered and stored in the refrigerator.

From the top: Nesting Eggs, Mustard Cheese Truffles

Clockwise from the top: Creamy Egg and Ham Ring, Salmon and Cucumber Mousses, Egg and Watercress Mousse

EGG AND WATERCRESS MOUSSES

Preparation time: 15 minutes, plus chilling
Serves 2

1 small bunch, about 100 g (4 oz) of
watercress, trimmed and sorted
2 hard-boiled eggs, shelled and finely
chopped
4 tablespoons low-calorie mayonnaise
3 tablespoons plain unsweetened yogurt
1 teaspoon powdered gelatine
1 teaspoon lemon juice
2 teaspoons water
salt
freshly ground black pepper
1 egg white

1. Reserve a few watercress sprigs to garnish and finely chop the remainder. Mix with the hard-boiled eggs, mayonnaise and yogurt.
2. Sprinkle the gelatine over the lemon juice and water and leave for five minutes until spongy. Stand it in a pan of hot water and gently stir with a metal spoon for about 5 minutes until clear. Fold into the watercress mixture with salt and pepper.
3. Whisk the egg white until it stands in stiff peaks and fold into the watercress mixture with a metal spoon. Spoon into 2 ramekin dishes and chill until set. [A]
4. Garnish each mousse with the reserved watercress sprigs.

[A] The mousses can be made up to 2 days in advance, covered and chilled.

SALMON AND CUCUMBER MOUSSES

Preparation time: 15 minutes, plus cooling and chilling

2 eggs, separated
2 teaspoons lemon juice
few drops of anchovy essence
salt
freshly ground white pepper
1 tablespoon powdered gelatine
150 ml (¼ pint) fish stock
225 g (8 oz) fresh or canned salmon, skin and bones removed
To garnish:
cucumber slices
8 tablespoons liquid aspic

1. Beat the egg yolks with the lemon juice, anchovy essence and salt and pepper over hot water until they thicken slightly. Allow to cool, beating lightly.
2. Dissolve the gelatine in the fish stock (see Egg and Watercress Mousses, opposite) and add to the egg mixture, blending well.
3. Flake the salmon and fold into the egg mixture.
4. Whisk the egg whites until they stand in stiff peaks and fold into the salmon mixture with a metal spoon. Pour into 4 small dishes and chill until set, about 30 minutes.
5. Top each mousse with a few of the cucumber slices and spoon over the aspic. Chill until set. [A]

[A] The mousses can be made up to 2 days in advance, if covered and chilled.

CREAMY EGG AND HAM RING

Preparation time: 20 minutes, plus chilling
Serves 6

7 tablespoons water
3 tablespoons lemon juice
15 g (½ oz) powdered gelatine
4 hard-boiled eggs, shelled
300 ml (½ pint) mayonnaise
225 g (8 oz) cooked ham, cut into fine julienne strips
150 ml (¼ pint) soured cream
1 tablespoon finely chopped fresh parsley
salt
freshly ground white pepper
To garnish:
watercress sprigs

1. Use 3 tablespoons of the water and the lemon juice with a heaped teaspoon of the gelatine and dissolve the gelatine (see Egg and Watercress Mousses, opposite). Pour into a lightly-oiled 900 ml (1½ pint) ring mould and chill until almost set.
2. Slice the hard-boiled eggs and arrange a layer in the base of the almost set mould. Chill until set.
3. Chop the remaining egg and mix with mayonnaise, ham, cream, parsley.
4. Dissolve the remaining gelatine in the remaining water and stir into the egg and ham mixture. Add salt and pepper to taste. Spoon into the ring mould, level the surface and chill for about 45 minutes until set. [A]
5. To serve, dip the mould briefly into hot water and invert on to a serving dish. Fill the centre with watercress.

[A] The ring can be made up to 3 days in advance, if covered and chilled.

HERB QUICHE

Preparation time: 25 minutes
Cooking time: 50 minutes
Oven: 200°C, 400°F, Gas Mark 6; then 180°C,
350°F, Gas Mark 4
Serves 4-6

350 g (12 oz) Basic shortcrust pastry
(see opposite)
1 egg yolk
Filling:
100 g (4 oz) sorrel
100 g (4 oz) spinach
50 g (2 oz) parsley
1 bunch watercress
4 tablespoons chopped mixed herbs:
tarragon, chervil, burnet and dill
2 eggs
300 ml (½ pint) single cream
salt
freshly ground black pepper
50 g (2 oz) freshly grated Parmesan cheese
To garnish:
sprigs of dill
fresh tarragon

1. Line a 23-25 cm (9-10 in.) flan tin with the pastry. Weigh down with foil and the pastry trimmings and bake for 10 minutes in a preheated moderately hot oven. Remove the foil and trimmings, brush the pastry all over with beaten egg yolk and put it back in the oven for a further 5 minutes. Take out and cool.
2. Wash and drain the sorrel, spinach, parsley and watercress. Put them all into a large pan of boiling water and boil for 4 minutes. Drain well, pressing out the moisture with the back of a wooden spoon. When the greens are cool enough to handle, squeeze out the liquid between your hands. Chop the drained greens and add the mixed herbs.
3. Beat the eggs in a bowl, add the cream and beat until blended, adding salt and pepper to taste and most of the grated Parmesan, reserving a little to scatter over the top. Mix the egg mixture with the chopped greenstuffs and pour into the pastry case. Scatter the reserved cheese over the top and bake for 30 minutes. Serve immediately with dill and tarragon.

MUSHROOMS IN PASTRY CASES

Preparation time: 25 minutes, plus chilling
Cooking time: 30 minutes
Oven: 190°C, 35°F, Gas Mark 5

350 g (12 oz) Basic shortcrust pastry
(see opposite)
450 g (1 lb) flat mushrooms
50 g (2 oz) butter
½ tablespoon plain flour
200 ml (⅓ pint) Chicken stock
(see page 14)
6 tablespoons sour cream
salt
freshy ground black pepper
lemon juice to taste
½ tablespoon chopped parsley
½ tablespoon chopped chives
½ tablespoon chopped tarragon
1 egg yolk

1. Chill the pastry for 30 minutes before using. Roll it out thinly and line four 7.5-10 cm/3-4 in round tin moulds. Lay a small piece of greased foil in each one, with a few pastry trimmings on it. Bake for 10 minutes in a preheated oven. Remove the foil and pastry and put the pans back in the oven for a further 5 minutes. Remove from the oven and leave to cool.
2. Wipe the mushrooms with a clean damp cloth and cut off the stalks. Slice the caps. Melt 40 g (1½ oz) butter in a covered pan. Cook the mushroom caps gently, stirring once or twice. When soft, drain off the juice and take the pan off the heat.
3. Melt the remaining butter in a saucepan and stir in the flour. Cook for 1 minute, stirring all the time. Add the heated stock and the sour cream, and cook for 3 minutes, stirring often. Add salt and pepper and lemon juice to taste, then mix in the drained mushrooms. Reheat the mixture and stir in the herbs.
4. Brush the pastry cases all over with beaten egg yolk and bake for a further 5 minutes in a preheated oven. Remove from the oven, fill with hot mushroom mixture and serve immediately.

BASIC SHORTCRUST PASTRY

Preparation time: 10 minutes
Cooking time: 15 minutes
Oven: 200°C, 400°F, Gas Mark 6
Makes sufficient to line one 20 cm (8-inch) flan tin

175 g (6 oz) plain flour
pinch of salt
75 g (3 oz) butter
2 tablespoons iced water

1. Sift the flour and salt into a bowl.
2. Rub in the butter with the fingertips until the mixture resembles fine breadcrumbs. Add the water and bind together to a firm but pliable dough.
3. Turn out on to a lightly floured surface; knead until smooth and free of cracks. Ⓐ
4. Roll out the pastry and use to line the flan tins of your choice. Ⓕ
5. To bake 'blind', prick the base well. Line the flan with greaseproof paper, then fill with baking beans. Place in a preheated oven and bake blind for 15 minutes.

Ⓐ Wrapped in cling film, the pastry may be stored in the refrigerator for 2-3 days.
Ⓕ Open freeze the uncooked flan case, then wrap in foil or a freezer bag. Freeze for up to 3 months. Cook from frozen, increasing the initial blind baking by 5-10 minutes.

From the left:
Mushrooms in Pastry
Cases, Herb Quiche

CHEESE AND TUNA OVEN-BAKED MUFFINS

Preparation time: 10 minutes
Cooking time: 15-20 minutes
Oven: 190°C, 375°F, Gas Mark 5

4 wholewheat or cheese muffins, split
1 onion, peeled and sliced into rings
2 × 184 g (6½ oz) cans tuna in brine,
drained and flaked
50 g (2 oz) alfalfa sprouts
3 tablespoons mayonnaise
3 tablespoons soured cream
2 tablespoons sunflower seeds
salt and freshly ground black pepper
75 g (3 oz) Cheddar cheese, grated
2 tomatoes, thinly sliced

1. Toast the muffins on their cut sides and place on a large baking sheet. Top each with an equal quantity of the onion.
2. Mix the tuna with the alfalfa mayonnaise, soured cream, sunflower seeds and salt and pepper to taste, blending well. Spread equally over the muffin slices. Sprinkle with the cheese and top each with a slice of tomato.
3. Bake in a preheated oven for 15-20 minutes, until golden, bubbly and heated through. Serve while still hot.

Illustrated on page 34

LAMBS' KIDNEYS IN PASTRY NESTS

Preparation time: 30 minutes
Cooking time: 45 minutes
Oven: 190°C, 375°F, Gas Mark 5
Serves 6

Pastry nests:
225 g (8 oz) Basic shortcrust pastry
(see page 43)
Filling:
40 g (1½ oz) butter
1 medium onion, peeled and finely
chopped
1 garlic clove, peeled and crushed
6 lambs' kidneys peeled, cored and thinly
sliced
15 g (½ oz) plain flour
150 ml (¼ pint) white wine
150 ml (¼ pint) stock
50 g (2 oz) button mushrooms, sliced
1 tablespoon chopped fresh parsley
2 tomatoes, skinned, pipped and diced
salt
freshly ground black pepper
parsley sprigs to garnish

1. To make the pastry nests, roll out the shortcrust pastry and use to line 6 individual foil containers (or ramekin dishes) each 6 cm (2½ inches) in diameter and 2.5 cm (1 inch) deep.
2. Line the pastry cases with greaseproof paper, then fill them with dried peas or lentils.
3. Bake blind in a preheated oven for 10 minutes.
4. Remove the paper with the peas or lentils, and return the pastry cases to the oven for 6-10 minutes until light golden in colour. Allow to cool then unmould.
5. To make the filling, melt the butter in a large shallow pan, and add the onion and garlic. Allow to cook gently until pale golden in colour. Add the kidneys to the pan, raise the heat and fry, stirring, for 2-3 minutes.
6. Remove the pan from the heat and stir in the flour, then the wine, stock, mushrooms and parsley. Return to the heat and simmer, stirring gently, for 8-10 minutes.
7. Add the tomatoes and salt and pepper, just allowing time for the tomatoes to warm through without breaking up.
8. When ready to serve, warm the pastry cases through and fill with the kidney mixture. Garnish with sprigs of parsley.

Lambs' Kidneys in Pastry Nests

FISH FOR STARTERS

Whatever your choice, from freshly cooked or smoked and oily or shell to canned or raw, here is a mariner's choice of fish to use in a wide range of starters.

If fresh is your choice you can feast on Skewered Monkfish or Seafood Mousse; if smoked is your fancy enjoy Finnan Cocottes or Smoked Haddock Soufflé; if oily is the order, opt for Fried Whitebait; if shell is your preference dine on Potted Shrimps, Lobster Salad or Prawn Puffs; if canned, try Tomatoes with Tuna Fish; or for raw, a fresh delight could be Gravad Lax or Ceviche of Scallops with Herbs.

To be enjoyed at their best, all types of fish should be at their peak of freshness when bought. Look for fish with a firm, not spongy, flesh; clear sparkling eyes; bright red gills; clean fresh smell; and undamaged appearance. Follow the seasons for economy, since every month brings its own fish speciality.

If you tend to avoid fish for fear of not knowing how to prepare it, then opt for those dishes that require minimum attention like Potted Cheese with Fish and Potted Shrimps. Later, you can progress to the more preparation-intensive dishes, but still leaving gutting, cleaning, filleting or shelling to the fishmonger.

The repertoire of fish dishes for starters is as wide as the cooking methods used to prepare them. You'll never tire of long-marinated fish slices and seafood; crisply deep-fried tiny fish cooked to a sizzle; puréed or beaten fish all the better for potting; golden-baked cocottes or soufflés with high-risen crowns; and skewered sticks of fish perfect for the grill or barbecue.

Fishy starters are best served before flavour-intensive main course dishes like sweetbreads cooked in cream with more than a dash of spirit; tender veal parcels stuffed with a herb-flavoured forcemeat; rabbit grilled with fiery mustard; or a curried or highly spiced meat dish, where their delicate flavour can be most appreciated. Round off such menus with a dazzling fresh fruit salad, simple fruit fool, fresh fruit jelly or a sorbet that will refresh the palate.

From the top: Smoked Haddock Soufflé (page 52), Ceviche of Scallops with Herbs (page 57), Fried Whitebait (page 51)

POTTED CHEESE WITH FISH

Preparation time: 10 minutes, plus chilling
Serves 4-6

175 g (6 oz) full-fat soft cheese
2 tablespoons milk
175 g (6 oz) smoked mackerel, skinned,
boned and flaked
1 tablespoon horseradish relish
2 tablespoons chopped parsley
4 tablespoons lemon juice
2 teaspoons powdered gelatine
2 egg whites
salt
freshly ground black pepper
To garnish:
parsley sprigs
wholemeal bread slices

1. Beat the cheese to soften then add the milk and beat until smooth. Add the mackerel, horseradish and parsley, blending well.
2. Place the lemon juice in a small bowl and sprinkle over the gelatine. Leave to soften, then place in a pan of hot water and leave until clear and dissolved.
3. Whisk the egg whites until they stand in stiff peaks. Beat the gelatine into the fish mixture with salt and pepper to taste. Fold in the egg whites then spoon into individual dishes or one large dish and chill to set.
4. Garnish with parsley sprigs and bread that has been cut into hearts using biscuit cutters then toasted until golden.

HUNDREDS AND THOUSANDS PÂTÉ

Preparation time: 30 minutes, plus setting
Cooking time: 3 minutes
Serves 6-8

225 g (8 oz) smoked cod's roe
225 g (8 oz) low fat soft cheese
2 tablespoons lemon juice
1 hard-boiled egg, finely chopped
1 tablespoon sunflower oil
freshly ground black pepper
8 tablespoons condensed consommé
1 tablespoon medium sherry
1 teaspoon powdered gelatine
To garnish:
chervil leaves
red and black lumpfish roe

1. Put the cod's roe in a bowl and pour on boiling water to cover. Drain the roe, cool slightly and peel off the skin. Mash the roe to break it up.
2. Mix together the roe, cheese, lemon juice, chopped egg and sunflower oil and beat well. Taste and season the mixture with pepper, then spoon into a serving dish.
3. Heat the consommé with the sherry, stir in the gelatine and dissolve. Set aside to cool.
4. When the gelatine mixture is like unbeaten egg white, spoon it over the pâté. Cover and put in the refrigerator to set.
5. Garnish the pâté with the herbs and the red and black lumpfish roe arranged like bunches of grapes.

FINNAN COCOTTES

Preparation time: 15 minutes
Cooking time: 45 minutes
Oven: 180°C, 350°F, Gas Mark 4

225 g (8 oz) smoked haddock fillet
2 bay leaves
6 black peppercorns
225 g (8 oz) cottage cheese
3 spring onions, chopped
100 g (4 oz) button mushrooms, chopped
2 eggs, beaten
1 tablespoon lemon juice
salt
freshly ground black pepper
3 tablespoons fresh wholemeal
breadcrumbs
1 tablespoon grated Parmesan cheese
1 teaspoon paprika
4 lemon slices, to garnish, (optional)

1. Place the fish in a pan with the bay leaves, peppercorns and just enough water to cover. Bring to the boil and simmer for 5 minutes. Drain, cool and flake the fish, removing the skin and any bones.
2. Mix the fish with the cottage cheese, onion and mushrooms. Stir in the beaten eggs and lemon juice and season with salt and pepper.
3. Divide the mixture between 4 greased cocotte dishes and level the tops. Mix together the breadcrumbs, cheese and paprika and sprinkle on top of each dish.
4. Stand the dishes in a roasting pan with water to come half-way up the sides. Cook in a preheated oven for 35 minutes, or until the mixture is just firm.
5. Serve hot, garnished with lemon slices, if liked, and accompanied by hot toast.

Clockwise from top left: Potted Cheese with Fish, Hundreds and Thousands Pâté, Finnan Cocottes, Prawn Puffs (page 50)

PRAWN PUFFS

Preparation time: 30 minutes
Cooking time: 30 minutes
Oven: 200°C, 400°F, Gas Mark 6
Serves 6

300 ml (½ pint) water
50 g (2 oz) margarine
100 g (4 oz) wholemeal flour
1 teaspoon dried mixed herbs
pinch of salt
2 large eggs
Filling:
225 g (8 oz) low fat soft chese
100 g (4 oz) shelled prawns, chopped
1 tablespoon chopped parsley
1 teaspoon lemon juice
pinch of cayenne
freshly ground black pepper

1. In a small pan, heat the water and margarine to boiling point. Stir together the flour, herbs and salt. Tip the fat mixture at once on to the flour and stir vigorously. Beat in the eggs one at a time, beating continuously.
2. Using 2 dessertspoons to shape rounds of the mixture, place them well apart on a greased baking tray.
3. Bake in a preheated oven for 15-20 minutes, or until the buns are well risen and sound hollow when tapped.
4. Split the buns open to allow the steam to escape and leave them on a wire rack to cool. Store for up to 1 day in an airtight tin.
5. Beat the filling ingredients together. Fill the buns just before serving and accompany with a salad garnish.

Illustrated on page 49

SEAFOOD MOUSSE

Preparation time: 20 minutes, plus cooling and setting
Cooking time: 20 minutes
Oven: 180°C, 350°F, Gas Mark 4
Serves 6-8

450 g (1 lb) salmon trout or 350 g (12 oz) middle cut of salmon
150 ml (¼ pint) dry white wine
150 ml (¼ pint) water
1 small onion, peeled and sliced
1 slice lemon
sprigs of parsley and thyme
1 bay leaf
salt
black peppercorns
Sauce:
25 g (1 oz) butter or margarine
25 g (1 oz) plain flour
300 ml (½ pint) cooking liquid
1 teaspoon lemon juice
1 teaspoon anchovy essence
1 egg, separated
150 ml (5 fl oz) plain unsweetened yogurt or soured cream
freshly ground black pepper
15 g (½ oz) powdered gelatine
green salad vegetables (cucumber, watercress), to garnish

1. Clean the fish and place in an ovenproof dish.
2. Pour the wine and water into a saucepan and add the flavourings. Bring to the boil and pour over the fish. Cover and bake in a preheated oven for 15-20 minutes until just cooked. Leave to cool.
3. Drain off the cooking liquid and make up to 300 ml (½ pint) with milk. Remove the head, tail, skin and bones from the fish, and flake the flesh.
4. For the sauce, melt the butter in a saucepan and stir in the flour. When blended, stir in the reserved cooking liquid and bring to the boil, stirring until thickened. Simmer for 2 minutes.
5. Place the flaked fish in a mixing bowl and stir the sauce in. Mix in the lemon juice, anchovy essence, egg yolk, and yogurt or soured cream. Add seasoning.
6. Dissolve the gelatine in 2 tablespoons of hot water and stir into the mousse. Whisk the egg white until stiff and fold in. Turn into a 900 ml (1½ pint) mould and chill until set. [A]
7. To serve, turn out on to a plate and garnish with salad vegetables. Green mayonnaise (see page 61) goes well with this mousse.

[A] The mousse can be made up to 1 day in advance, covered and kept chilled.

FRIED WHITEBAIT

Preparation time: 10 minutes
Cooking time: 12-15 minutes

500 g (1 lb) whitebait
100 g (4 oz) plain flour
salt
freshly ground black pepper
oil for deep frying
To garnish:
1 lemon, quartered
few sprigs of watercress

Illustrated on page 46

1. Sort through the whitebait, discarding any crushed or broken ones. If it is necessary to wash the fish, use ice cold water and carefully pat them dry on a tea towel.
2. Spread the flour on a sheet of paper and season with salt and pepper. Heat the oil to 190°C (375°F). Take a quarter of the fish and toss them in the flour, making sure they are well covered. Transfer them to the frying basket and shake off any surplus flour. Plunge the basket into the oil for 2 minutes. Drain the fish on kitchen paper and fry the remaining three batches.
3. When all the fish is cooked check the oil temperature and tip all the whitebait into the frying basket. Plunge the basket into the oil to re-heat and crisp the fish, about 2 minutes. Drain the fish on kitchen paper, then pile them on to a serving dish and garnish with lemon and watercress.
4. Serve with thin brown bread and butter.

Seafood Mousse

SMOKED HADDOCK SOUFFLÉ

Preparation time: 15 minutes
Cooking time: 40-45 minutes
Oven: 190°C, 375°F, Gas Mark 5

50 g (2 oz) butter
2 tablespoons grated Parmesan cheese
40 g (1½ oz) plain flour
300 ml (½ pint) milk
2 tablespoons lemon juice
1 teaspoon mustard powder
salt
freshly ground black pepper
4 eggs, separated
225 g (8 oz) smoked haddock, cooked,
skinned, boned and flaked

1. Grease a 20 cm (8 inch) soufflé dish with a quarter of the butter. Add the Parmesan cheese to the dish and shake gently to coat the base and sides.
2. Melt the remaining butter in a pan. Add the flour and cook for 1 minute. Gradually add the milk, blending well. Bring to the boil and cook for 2-3 minutes, stirring constantly. Add the lemon juice, mustard and salt and pepper, blending well. Allow to cool slightly, then beat in the egg yolks and blend in the fish.
3. Whisk the egg whites until they stand in stiff peaks. Fold into the sauce with a metal spoon. Pour into the prepared soufflé dish and cook in a preheated moderately hot oven for 30-35 minutes or until well-risen and golden.
4. Serve at once, with mixed salad.

Illustrated on page 46

TOMATOES WITH TUNA FISH

Preparation time: 15 minutes

4 large tomatoes
1 × 225 g (8 oz) can tuna fish, drained
150 ml (¼ pint) mayonnaise
salt
freshly ground black pepper
1 teaspoon finely chopped fresh parsley

This is another dish which could be used for lunch or supper, served with a salad.
1. Place the tomatoes stalk side down and, with a sharp knife, cut 4 or 5 slices down through each one, leaving it joined at the base, so that it opens out like the leaves of a book.
2. With a fork, blend the tuna fish well with 1 tablespoon of the mayonnaise and the salt and pepper. It can be left coarsely mixed, or blended to a smooth paste according to personal preference.
3. Spoon the fish mixture into each slit in the tomatoes.
4. If the mayonnaise is very stiff, mix it with a little hot water to give a firm coating consistency. If liked, coat the top of each tomato with a spoonful of the remaining mayonnaise and sprinkle with a little chopped parsley.

Variation: Salmon or sardines can be used instead of tuna fish.

AVOCADOS AND CRAB

Preparation time: 15 minutes

2 medium to large ripe avocados
1 tablespoon lemon juice
225 g (8 oz) white crab meat, flaked
150 ml (¼ pint) mayonnaise
2-3 teaspoons tomato purée or ketchup
2-3 drops Tabasco sauce
1 teaspoon finely chopped fresh parsley or
chives

1. Cut the avocados in half and remove the stone. With a teaspoon, carefully remove the flesh from the skins and cut into dice.
2. Mix the flesh with the lemon juice to prevent discoloration and replace in the skins, leaving a small well in the centre.
3. Pile the crab meat in the avocado centres, heaping it up as much as possible.
4. Blend the mayonnaise with sufficient tomato purée or ketchup to colour and flavour, and add the Tabasco sauce to taste.
5. Coat the crab with the sauce and sprinkle with a little chopped parsley or chives.

From the left: Avocados and Crab, Tomatoes with Tuna Fish

POTTED SHRIMPS

Preparation time: 10 minutes, plus overnight cooling
Cooking time: 10 minutes
Serves 6

450 g (1 lb) shelled shrimps or prawns
1 teaspoon ground mace
225 g (8 oz) butter
salt
¼ teaspoon cayenne pepper

1. Finely chop half the shellfish and mix the two lots together with the mace.
2. Melt 175 g (6 oz) of the butter in a pan, but do not let it boil. Stir in the shellfish and then add salt and cayenne pepper to taste. Stir over low heat until all the butter is absorbed into the mixture.
3. Turn into small jars or moulds and press well down. Melt the remaining butter and pour over the top of each mould, while the mixture is still hot.
4. Leave in the refrigerator at least overnight before using. A F Turn out on a plate and serve with very hot dry toast.

A This will keep for 3 to 4 weeks in the refrigerator.
F Can be frozen for 3 months. Thaw overnight in the refrigerator or a cool room, taking care that the butter does not melt too much.

LOBSTER SALAD

Preparation time: 30 minutes, plus chilling

1 large lobster, meat removed and coral and claws saved or
2 small ones prepared in the same way
¼ teaspoon salt
freshly ground black pepper
150 ml (¼ pint) good mayonnaise
1 large crisp lettuce
4 tablespoons French dressing
3 hard-boiled eggs, cut in quarters longways
1 tablespoon finely chopped parsley

Lobster is very expensive and its delicious flavour is so delicate that it should have no strong-tasting accompaniments. Crisp lettuce sets it off best without other salad vegetables. The mayonnaise should be a good make or home-made and can have one tablespoon double cream stirred into it, if it seems too sharp-tasting.
1. Chop all the claw meat, season with salt and pepper and reserve. Chop the rest of the lobster meat and mix it with the coral and the mayonnaise.
2. Remove the outer leaves and stems from the lettuce and chop all but about a quarter.
3. Dress the chopped lettuce with French dressing and pile in the centre of a flat serving dish. Pile the lobster meat on top, arrange the remaining lettuce leaves around the sides with the claw meat.
4. Arrange the egg quarters so that they resemble flower petals. Garnish with the claws and sprinkle parsley over all. Chill before serving.

SEAFOOD-STUFFED FRENCH BREAD

Preparation time: 15 minutes
Cooking time: 15 minutes
Oven: 180°C, 250°F, Gas Mark 4

2 small French loaves
freshly ground black pepper
salt
275 g (10 oz) peeled prawns or crab meat
75 g (3 oz) butter
Forcemeat:
50 g (2 oz) suet
2 teaspoons chopped thyme and parsley
salt
freshly ground black pepper
1 egg
100 g (4 oz) fine white breadcrumbs (may
be made from the inside of the loaves)
1 tablespoon stock (cube will do)

1. Cut off one end from each loaf and reserve. Scoop out all the crumb.
2. Make the forcemeat by mixing all the ingredients well together.
3. Rub the loaves lightly all over with a grater so that the outside is roughened. Reserve a little of the forcemeat for the ends and spread the remainder on the inside of the loaves. Fill the loaves with the prawns or crab meat. Spread the ends of the loaves with forcemeat and press back into place.
4. Melt the butter in a frying pan and fry the loaves in the hot butter, turning frequently, until a golden brown on all sides. Remove and drain on paper towels.
5. Put the loaves on a baking sheet in a preheated oven for 10 minutes, to heat through. Serve at once, cutting the loaves in half crossways.

Clockwise from the top:
Lobster Salad, Seafood-Stuffed French Bread, Potted Shrimps

SKEWERED MONKFISH

Preparation time: 25 minutes
Cooking time: about 15 minutes

750 g (1½ lb) monkfish tails or large peeled
scampi
about 12 bay leaves
2 tablespoons melted butter
salt
freshly ground white pepper
Sauce:
4 teaspoons cornflour
250 ml (8 fl oz) cold water
grated rind of 1 lemon
25 g (1 oz) butter
3 tablespoons lemon juice
1 egg yolk
3 tablespoons medium sherry
2 tablespoons double cream
salt
freshly ground white pepper

1. Prepare the monkfish tails by removing the flesh, in 2 pieces, from the central bone and slice into bite-sized 'medallions'.
2. Thread the monkfish, or scampi, on to 4 short skewers, alternating with the bay leaves. Brush with the melted butter and sprinkle with salt and pepper to taste.
3. Place on a grill rack and cook under a preheated hot grill for 12-15 minutes, until cooked, turning frequently.
4. Meanwhile, place the cornflour in a pan and stir in the cold water. Add the lemon rind and butter and bring to the boil, stirring constantly. Cook for 2 minutes, then remove from the heat.
5. Beat the lemon juice with the egg yolk. Add a little of the hot sauce, then return to the sauce in the pan, blending well. Heat gently until hot but not boiling. Stir in the sherry and cream with salt and pepper to taste.
6. Serve at once spooning a little of the sauce over the monkfish or scampi kebabs and serving the rest separately.

Skewered Monkfish,
Gravad Lax

CEVICHE OF SCALLOPS WITH HERBS

Preparation time: 20 minutes, plus marinating

10 large scallops
4 scallop shells
150 ml (¼ pint) lemon juice
1½ tablespoons chopped shallot
½ tablespoon chopped tarragon
½ tablespoon chopped dill
½ tablespoon chopped chives
½ tablespoon chopped parsley
1½ tablespoons sunflower-seed oil
sprigs of parsley, to garnish

Illustrated on page 46

1. Detach the scallops from their shells and scrape off the beard-like fringe and intestinal thread. Cut away the orange flesh. Wash the white parts and pat dry. Cut in slices about 5 mm (¼ inch) thick. Wash and prepare the coral in the same way, if you like.
2. Choose 4 medium shells, scrub them well and leave to drain.
3. Put the sliced scallops in a bowl and pour over the lemon juice. (There should be enough almost to cover them.) Cover with cling film and put in the refrigerator for 24 hours, stirring occasionally.
4. When ready to serve, chop the shallots and the herbs very finely indeed. Drain off the lemon juice from the scallops and stir in the oil. Add the shallots and herbs and mix well. Spoon on to the shells and serve immediately, garnished with parsley, and with brown bread and butter.

GRAVAD LAX

Preparation time: 30 minutes, plus pressing
Serves 6-8

1 × 1 kg (2¼ lb) piece middle-cut fresh salmon
65 g (2½ oz) caster sugar
large bunch of fresh dill, finely chopped
65 g (2½ oz) coarse sea salt
10 black peppercorns, crushed
Sauce:
2 tablespoons German mustard
1 egg yolk
1 tablespoon caster sugar
2 tablespoons white wine vinegar
7 tablespoons olive or salad oil
1 tablespoon chopped fresh dill
salt
freshly ground black pepper
To garnish:
lemon slices
sprig of fresh dill

1. Wash, then thoroughly dry, the salmon. Skin and remove any bones to make 2 large fillets. Rub the sugar all over the fish.
2. Sprinkle a little of the dill on the base of a large shallow dish. Top with one of the salmon fillets. Sprinkle with a little more of the dill, half the sea salt and all the crushed peppercorns. Cover with the remaining salmon fillet, remaining sea salt and some of the dill.
3. Place a wooden chopping board on top, with a piece of cling film in between, and weight heavily to press the salmon fillets firmly together. Chill, for at least 48 hours. [A]
4. To make the sauce, beat the mustard with the egg yolk, caster sugar and vinegar. Slowly beat in the oil, drop by drop, until thickened and well blended. Add some chopped dill, reserving a little for the garnish, and salt and pepper to taste.
5. To serve, slice the salmon paper-thin and pour over a little of the mustard sauce. Garnish with the reserved chopped dill, lemon slices and fresh dill.
6. Gravad lax is delicious served with buttered rye or wholemeal bread. Serve with lager or cold schnapps.

[A] The salmon fillets can be chilled for up to 5 days at this stage.

VEGETABLES & SALADS

From the richly exotic aubergine to the humble cabbage, the elegant asparagus to the homely leek, vegetables and salad ingredients make simple and inexpensive starters.

Salad lovers who appreciate greenery can feast for starters on Courgette Timbale Salad in the spring; Midsummer Salad in the height of summer; Tuscan Nectarine and Avocado Salad in early autumn; and Cottage Cheese Salad in the depths of winter. And those who think salads are for the rabbits should look again at Moussaka Salad with its lashings of lamb or beef, Spinach and Smoked Ham Salad with its satisfying selection of ham, cheese and rich avocado, or Tuna Bean Salad with tender flakes of tuna and colourful array of hearty broad and red kidney beans.

Vegetables make a wonderfully versatile start to any meal. Served simply like Asparagus with Green Mayonnaise, a little more adventurously like Leeks à la Grecque, or splendidly adventurously like Celery and Walnut Roll, there is a recipe to suit every occasion, every palate and every cook. Indeed, health-conscious cooks will also take note that they are serving perhaps one of the better balanced starters to a meal for vegetables are generally low in calories, rich in vitamins and vital minerals, low in cholesterol and score highly in the fibre stakes. Many also make a valuable, cheap contribution to the protein we require in our diets.

These generally lighter vegetable and salad starters can be served before more substantial main courses like roast lamb garnished with cooked haricot or flageolet beans, rich braised oxtail, Coq au Vin, marmalade-basted duck, meat and pasta lasagne or cheese-crusted Moussaka, especially if you choose a light dessert such as a citrus mousse, berry sorbet, fruit and yogurt whip or simple summer fruit salad to complete the meal.

From the top: Leeks à la Grecque (page 61), Moussaka Salad (page 60)

MOUSSAKA SALAD

Preparation time: 20 minutes, plus standing
Cooking time: 30-50 minutes
Oven: 180°C, 350°F, Gas Mark 4

750 g (1¾ lb) aubergines, stalks removed
1 tablespoon salt
about 150 ml (¾ pint) oil
1 large onion, peeled and chopped
750 g (1½ lb) minced lamb or beef
1 teaspoon tomato purée
1 garlic clove, peeled and crushed
(optional)
freshly ground black pepper
1 large tomato, thinly sliced
3 eggs
1 tablespoon fresh marjoram or ½ teaspoon
dried

Illustrated on page 58

1. Cut the aubergines into thin slices about 3 mm (⅛ inch) thick. Put them in a colander, sprinkle with the salt and leave to drain for 30 minutes.
2. Rinse the aubergine slices and pat dry.
3. Heat 3 tablespoons of oil in a large frying pan. Fry the aubergine slices in batches until golden brown on both sides, adding 6 tablespoons of oil as necessary. Remove the slices with a slotted spoon.
4. Gently fry the onion in the last tablespoon of oil for 5 minutes. Add the minced meat and fry for 5-10 minutes, stirring until browned. Add the tomato purée, garlic, and a little salt and pepper.
5. Lightly grease a 1.25 litre (2 pint) ovenproof dish, or 4 individual 300 ml (½ pint) dishes. Arrange the aubergine slices, overlapping, over the base and sides of the dish, reserving some for the top. Arrange the tomato slices on top.
6. Spoon the mince mixture into the dish. Beat the eggs with the marjoram, pepper and a little salt. Pour the eggs over the mince and cover with the remaining aubergine slices.
7. Bake for 30 minutes in a large dish and for 15-20 minutes in smaller dishes, until the egg is set. Leave to cool. [A]
8. Run a palette knife around the edge of the dish(es) and invert on to a serving plate. Accompany with endive leaves.

[A] Can be prepared up to 2 days ahead, covered and kept chilled.

Asparagus with Green Mayonnaise

LEEKS À LA GRECQUE

Preparation time: 15 minutes
Cooking time: 30 minutes

300 ml (½ pint) water (or water and dry
white wine mixed)
2 tablespoons olive oil
grated rind of 1 lemon
2 tablespoons lemon juice
1 shallot or small onion, peeled and thinly
sliced
1 small stick celery with leaves
sprig of parsley
sprig of thyme or ¼ teaspoon dried thyme
1 bay leaf
¼ teaspoon salt
6 peppercorns
6 coriander seeds or ¼ teaspoon ground
coriander
450 g (1 lb) leeks

Illustrated on page 58

1. Pour the water, or water and wine, into a large saucepan and add the olive oil, lemon rind and juice, shallot or onion, celery and leaves, parsley, thyme, bay leaf, salt, peppercorns and coriander. Cover the pan, bring to the boil and simmer for 10 minutes.
2. Cut off the roots of the leeks and the ragged green leaves at the top, so that each leek measures about 18 cm (7 inches) long.
3. Make a long, lengthways cut in each leek, starting at the green end. Pull the leaves open and plunge the leeks, green ends first, into cold water to flush out any grit from the insides.
4. Place the prepared leeks in the simmering water, cover and simmer for 10-15 minutes until the leeks are tender.
5. Remove the leeks from the pan with a slotted spoon and place on a serving dish.
6. Boil the remaining liquid to reduce to about 150 ml (¼ pint). Pour the liquid over the leeks (removing the herbs and spices if preferred). Leave to cool. A

A The leeks can be prepared up to 1 day in advance, covered and kept chilled.

ASPARAGUS WITH GREEN MAYONNAISE

Preparation time: 30 minutes, plus cooling
Cooking time: 20-25 minutes
Serves 6

2 bundles asparagus
Green mayonnaise:
3 egg yolks
1 tablespoon finely chopped chives
1 tablespoon finely chopped fresh parsley
1 tablespoon lemon juice
300 ml (½ pint) olive oil
salt
freshly ground black pepper

1. Wash the asparagus and trim the ends. Scrape the lower half of each spear, then divide into 6 bundles.
2. Tie each bunch firmly, finishing with a long-ended bow. (This makes it easier to remove the string after cooking.)
3. Fill a large pan with salted water and bring to the boil. If you have a pan deep enough for the spears to stand upright, so much the better, and the tender points can then be above the water level. This means that they are steamed while the firmer parts of the stalks are cooking in the water.
4. Place the lid on the pan, and boil until just tender. Do not overcook.
5. Carefully remove the bundles and place them on a wire tray to drain and go cold.
6. To make the sauce, place the yolks, herbs and lemon juice in a liquidizer or food processor and mix for 1-2 minutes. Keeping the motor running, pour in the oil in a very thin stream until all is incorporated. Add salt and pepper.
7. To serve, untie the bundles of asparagus and place 1 bundle on each plate. Serve the sauce separately and accompany the dish with Melba toast.

BAKED FENNEL COCOTTES

Preparation time: 10 minutes
Cooking time: 30-35 minutes
Oven: 190°C, 375°F, Gas Mark 5

2 tablespoons oil
1 onion, peeled and chopped
2 bulbs fennel, trimmed and thickly sliced
225 g (8 oz) canned chopped tomatoes
1 × 220 g (7 oz) can butter beans, drained
2 tablespoons chopped parsley
salt
freshly ground black pepper
50 g (2 oz) wholemeal breadcrumbs
2 tablespoons sunflower seeds (optional)
25 g (1 oz) peanuts, chopped

1. Heat the oil in a pan. Add the onion and fennel and cook gently until softened, about 10 minutes.
2. Add the tomatoes, beans, half the parsley and salt and pepper to taste, blending well. Heat gently until hot then divide equally between four large individual ovenproof cocottes or dishes.
3. Mix the breadcrumbs with the remaining parsley, sunflower seeds if used, peanuts and salt and pepper to taste. Sprinkle over the fennel mixture.
4. Bake in a preheated oven for 20-25 minutes until the fennel mixture is cooked and tender and the topping is crisp and golden. Serve hot.

Variation: Baked Aubergine Cocottes: prepare and cook as above but use 1 large thickly cubed aubergine instead of the fennel. The aubergine should be sprinkled with a little salt and left to drain in a sieve for about 20 minutes then rinsed and dried before using to prevent bitterness.

Clockwise from top left: Spinach and Smoked Ham with Blue Cheese Dressing, Baked Fennel Cocottes, Tuscan Nectarine and Avocado Salad

SPINACH AND SMOKED HAM WITH BLUE CHEESE DRESSING

Preparation time: 15 minutes
Serves 4-6

275 g (10 oz) fresh spinach leaves, washed and stalks removed
225 g (8 oz) cooked smoked ham, cut into thin strips
1 large ripe avocado, halved, peeled, stoned and sliced
1 tablespoon lemon juice
Dressing:
100 g (4 oz) blue cheese, crumbled
150 ml (¼ pint) mayonnaise

1. Shred the spinach leaves finely and place in a large salad or serving dish. Add half of the ham and toss to mix.
2. Mix the avocado with the lemon juice and arrange attractively over the spinach and ham mixture.
3. To make the dressing, place the cheese in a bowl and beat until smooth and creamy. Gradually blend in the mayonnaise to make a smooth and thickened dressing. Spoon over the avocado and sprinkle with the remaining ham.
4. Serve lightly chilled.

TUSCAN NECTARINE AND AVOCADO SALAD

Preparation time: 10 minutes

2 fresh nectarines, blanched and peeled
1 ripe avocado, halved and stoned
225 g (8 oz) mixed salad leaves (curly endive, lamb's lettuce, radicchio and chicory for example)
8-12 small cherry tomatoes
Dressing:
5 tablespoons olive oil
5 teaspoons tarragon vinegar
1 garlic clove, peeled and crushed
1 teaspoon wholegrain mustard
1 teaspoon chopped fresh tarragon
1 teaspoon snipped chives
salt
freshly ground black pepper

1. Slice the nectarines thinly and place in a large salad bowl. Cut the avocado into small balls using a melon baller or teaspoon and add to the nectarines. Add the mixed salad leaves and tomatoes, turning over gently to blend.
2. To make the dressing, beat the oil and vinegar together until well blended and lightly thickened. Add the garlic, mustard, tarragon, chives and salt and pepper to taste, blending well. Spoon over the salad and toss lightly to mix.
3. Serve at once with chunks of wholemeal or granary bread.

COURGETTE TIMBALE SALAD

Preparation time: 15 minutes
Cooking time: 50 minutes (35 minutes if cooking as a starter in smaller moulds)
Oven: 180°C, 350°F, Gas Mark 4
Serves 4 as a light main salad or 8 as a starter

750 g (1½ lb) courgettes, sliced
1 tablespoon chopped fresh basil or mint
4 eggs, beaten
150 ml (5 fl oz) single cream or milk
salt
freshly ground black pepper
2 tablespoons grated Parmesan cheese
To serve:
4 tomatoes, thinly sliced
1 carton mustard and cress
2-3 tablespoons French dressing

1. Cook the courgettes in boiling water for 5 minutes.
2. Drain, add the chopped herbs and purée in a liquidizer, food processor or mouli-légumes.
3. Stir the beaten eggs into the courgette purée with the cream or milk. Add plenty of salt and pepper.
4. Pour into 4 well-greased 300 ml (½ pint) ramekins. Sprinkle each with Parmesan and bake in a preheated oven for about 45 minutes until set. (For a starter bake in 8 × 150 ml (¼ pint) ramekins for 20-30 minutes.) Leave to cool, then chill. $\boxed{A}$
5. Turn the timbales out on to individual plates. Surround with the tomato slices and the mustard and cress. Spoon the French dressing over.

$\boxed{A}$ Can be made up to 1 day in advance, covered and kept chilled.

MIDSUMMER SALAD

Preparation time: 15 minutes

1 small ripe melon
100 g (4 oz) strawberries, hulled
1 × 7.5 cm (3 inch) piece cucumber
1 small crisp lettuce, shredded
4 tablespoons French dressing
2 tablespoons chopped fresh mint
salt
freshly ground black pepper
15 g (½ oz) flaked almonds, to garnish

1. Cut the melon into quarters, then remove the seeds and skin. Cut the flesh into cubes, about 1 cm (½ inch) square, or scoop into balls.
2. Cut the strawberries and cucumber into thin slices.
3. To serve, arrange the shredded lettuce on a large serving dish or 4 individual plates. Arrange the pieces of melon, strawberry and cucumber on the lettuce.
4. Mix the French dressing with the chopped mint and add salt and pepper. Pour over the salad just before serving, and sprinkle with the almonds. As a side salad this goes very well with a selection of hard and soft cheeses, or ham.

Variations: Use small ogen melons, allowing half a melon per person. Arrange the salad in the scooped out melon halves. Substitute sliced banana or kiwi fruit for some or all of the strawberries.

COTTAGE CHEESE
SALAD

Preparation time: 15 minutes

450 g (1 lb) cottage cheese
1 × 7.5 cm (3 inch) piece cucumber, diced
225 g (8 oz) dates, stoned
350 g (12 oz) white cabbage or Chinese
leaves, cored and shredded
2 large carrots, peeled and coarsely grated
4 spring onions, chopped or 1 tablespoon
grated onion
2 red eating apples, cored and chopped
4 tablespoons French dressing
lettuce leaves
parsley springs, to garnish

If using Chinese leaves for this recipe a few whole leaves may be used in place of the bed of lettuce leaves.

1. Put the cottage cheese and cucumber into a bowl. Reserve four dates for the garnish; roughly chop the remainder and mix with the cottage cheese. Combine the cabbage or Chinese leaves, carrots and onions.

2. Dip the apples in the French dressing, then fold into the cabbage mixture.

3. Arrange a bed of lettuce leaves on a flat serving dish and top with the cabbage mixture, keeping it fairly flat. Spoon the cottage cheese mixture across the centre and garnish with the reserved whole dates and parsley sprigs.

Illustrated on page 66

From the top:
*Midsummer Salad with a
selection of cheeses,
Courgette Timbale Salad*

Clockwise from the left:
Cottage Cheese Salad
(page 65), Red Bean and
Carrot Salad, Tuna Bean
Salad, Sweetcorn and
Bean-Sprout Salad

SWEETCORN AND
BEAN-SPROUT SALAD

Preparation time: about 8 minutes

1 × 300 g (11 oz) can sweetcorn kernels,
drained
1 × 300 g (11 oz) can bean-sprouts, drained
or 8 oz fresh bean-sprouts, blanched for 1
minute and drained
8 spring onions, chopped
4 tablespoons French dressing
1 tablespoon soy sauce
salt
freshly ground black pepper
spinach leaves, torn into pieces

1. Mix together all the ingredients, except
the spinach, seasoning to taste with salt
and pepper. Line a salad bowl with
spinach and spoon the corn salad on top.

RED BEAN AND CARROT SALAD

Preparation time: 10 minutes

1 × 200 g (7 oz) can sweetcorn kernels,
drained
1 × 425 g (15 oz) can red kidney beans,
drained
1 tablespoon finely chopped onion or
spring onion
8-12 oz carrots, peeled, diced and cooked
4 tablespoons French dressing
salt
freshly ground black pepper
lettuce leaves

1. Mix together all the ingredients, except the lettuce, seasoning to taste with salt and pepper. Spoon on to a bed of lettuce to serve.

TUNA BEAN SALAD

Preparation time: 15 minutes

225 g (8 oz) frozen broad beans, cooked
and cooled
1 × 425 g (15 oz) can red kidney beans,
drained and rinsed under cold running
water
1 × 200 g (7 oz) can tuna fish, drained and
roughly flaked
2 tablespoons chopped fresh chives
1 × 5 cm (2 inch) piece cucumber, diced
4 celery sticks, sliced
1 eating apple, quartered, cored and
chopped
4-6 tablespoons French dressing
grated rind of ½ lemon
lettuce leaves (optional)
To garnish:
lemon slices
cucumber slices

This salad, without the lettuce, will keep in a cool place for several hours before serving.
1. Put the broad beans and kidney beans in a bowl with the tuna fish, chives, cucumber and celery. Toss the apple in the French dressing with the lemon rind added.
2. Mix thoroughly with the rest of the salad ingredients and serve in a salad bowl.
3. If preferred the salad may be arranged on a bed of crisp lettuce. Garnish with lemon and cucumber slices.

Variation: Use 175 g (6 oz) dried, red kidney beans instead of canned. Soak the beans overnight, drain and cook them in unsalted boiling water for 2-2½ hours until well cooked.

KITCHEN-GARDEN LOAF

Preparation time: 45 minutes
Cooking time: 1¾ hours
Oven: 180°C, 350°F, Gas Mark 4
Serves 6-8

2 medium carrots, scraped and cut into
matchstick strips
175 g (6 oz) asparagus spears
175 g (6 oz) French beans, topped and
tailed
salt
25 g (1 oz) soft margarine
1 medium onion, peeled and chopped
1 garlic clove, peeled and crushed
225 g (8 oz) button mushrooms, chopped
(reserve 2 for garnish)
225 g (8 oz) cottage cheese
50 g (2 oz) Roquefort cheese, crumbled
4 eggs
150 ml (¼ pint) plain unsweetened yogurt
1 tablespoon chopped fresh parsley
½ teaspoon dried thyme
¼ teaspoon grated nutmeg
freshly ground black pepper
1 hard-boiled egg, sliced, to garnish
Dressing:
150 ml (¼ pint) plain unsweetened yogurt
1 teaspoon French mustard
½ teaspoon curry powder
2 tablespoons double cream
1 teaspoon lemon juice

1. Cook the carrots, asparagus and beans in boiling, salted water until they are just tender. Drain and plunge at once into cold water to prevent further cooking. Drain again. Pat dry.
2. Grease a 1 kg (2 lb) loaf tin and line it with greased greaseproof paper.
3. Melt the margarine and gently fry the onion and garlic for 3 minutes, stirring. Add the mushrooms and cook for 3 minutes.
4. Blend the onion mixture with the cheese, eggs, yogurt and parsley. Add the thyme and nutmeg and season.
5. Pour one quarter of the egg and cheese mixture into the prepared tin. Lay the asparagus spears over them lengthways along the tin. Pour in one third of the remaining mixture and top with a layer of carrots. Pour on one half of the remaining mixture, top with a layer of beans then pour on the rest of the egg.
6. Stand in a roasting tin half filled with water. Cover with foil. Place in a preheated oven and bake for 1½ hours, or until the egg custard is set. Cool the tin on a wire rack, then chill.
7. Turn the loaf out on to a plate. Garnish with slices of egg and the reserved mushrooms. Leave at room temperature for 30 minutes.
8. To make the dressing, mix all the ingredients together and serve chilled.

CELERY AND WALNUT ROLL

Preparation time: 25 minutes
Cooking time: 30 minutes
Oven: 200°C, 400°F, Gas Mark 6

4 eggs, separated
75 g (3 oz) Gruyère cheese, grated
2 teaspoons celery seed
4 tablespoons celery leaves, finely chopped
Filling:
175 g (6 oz) low fat soft cheese
75 g (3 oz) walnuts, chopped
2 tablespoons chopped flat-leaved parsley
freshly ground black pepper
celery leaves, to garnish

1. Line a Swiss roll tin with greased greaseproof paper.
2. Beat the egg yolks until they are creamy, then beat in 25 g (1 oz) of the cheese, celery seed and celery leaves.
3. Whisk the egg whites until stiff and fold them into the celery mixture. Spread the mixture over the tin and level the top.
4. Place in a preheated oven and bake for 25 minutes, or until firm to the touch.
5. Beat together the soft cheese, walnuts and parsley and season with pepper.
6. Remove the tin from the oven. Spread the filling over the sponge. Using the paper to lift it up, roll it up from one short end.
7. Lift the roll on to a heatproof dish. Sprinkle the remaining cheese on top and return it to the oven for 3-4 minutes to melt the cheese. Serve hot, garnished with celery leaves.

CABBAGE BASKET

Preparation time: 1 hour
Cooking time: 1¾ hours

1 small white or green cabbage
salt
450 g (1 lb) carrots
50 g (2 oz) soft margarine
1 medium onion, peeled and chopped
1 garlic clove, peeled and crushed
1 teaspoon ground ginger
1 tablespoon clear honey
100 g (4 oz) cooked brown rice
100 g (4 oz) hazelnuts, chopped
freshly ground black pepper
40 g (1½ oz) fresh wholewheat
breadcrumbs
1 hard-boiled egg, finely chopped
1 tablespoon chopped fresh parsley

1. Remove any damaged or discoloured outer leaves from the cabbage and trim to a neat shape. Blanch in boiling, salted water for 5 minutes. Drain thoroughly.
2. Cook the carrots in boiling, salted water. Drain, reserving the liquid, and chop finely.
3. With 2 large spoons, gently pull a few leaves of the cabbage outwards, to expose the centre leaves and stalk. Remove these, leaving 'walls' about 2.5 cm (1 inch) thick. Finely chop the centre leaves.
4. Melt half the margarine and fry the onion and garlic over moderate heat for 3 minutes, stirring once or twice. Stir in the chopped cabbage, carrots, ginger, honey, rice, half the hazelnuts and 4 tablespoons of the reserved carrot stock. Season, remove from the heat and stir well.
5. Pack the filling into the cabbage 'basket' and wrap it lightly in foil.
6. Stand the cabbage on a trivet in a pan of fast-boiling water, reduce the heat, cover the pan and cook for 1½ hours.
7. Melt the remaining margarine and fry the breadcrumbs and reserved nuts. Stir in the egg and parsley.
8. Transfer the cabbage to a heated serving dish and sprinkle the crumb mixture on top. Serve hot, cut into wedges.

Clockwise from the left:
Cabbage Basket,
Kitchen-Garden Loaf,
Celery and Walnut Roll

PASTA, RICE & PANCAKES

In contrast to the vegetables of the previous chapter, the recipes here make, on the whole, substantial, even hearty dishes.

Rice in all its forms from long, short or round-grain; brown, white or wild; and pre-cooked American style, Italian risotto or Indian basmati, makes a good starter before a light main meal. Combined with chicken or scampi in a risotto it could indeed be mistaken for the main course, so keep portions small and under control.

Pasta and pancakes can suffer from the same delusions of heartiness, especially when coated or stuffed with rich sauces, sprinkled with lashings of cheese or layered with rich meat and vegetable combinations. All, however, prove wonderfully cooperative ingredients for the busy cook who needs to cook ahead, freeze or chill then reheat; the easy-going hostess who hates to clockwatch and seat guests at a moment's notice or the dish will spoil; and the economical or cooking-for-a-crowd chef who knows the purse strings or budget must not be stretched unduly.

These are certainly the starters to serve with light or nouvelle cuisine-style main courses like simple but succulent grilled lamb cutlets with fruity sauce, steamed fillets or baby steaks of fresh fish like salmon, turbot or sole with a hint of mayonnaise or hollandaise sauce, or slivered slices of chicken breasts served with a colourful nest of julienne vegetables. Most menus will then only require the temptation of a seemingly light but wicked dessert like chocolate profiteroles, fruit-filled individual tarts, or a thin slice of strudel to prove unforgettable.

Rice, pasta and pancakes may be magnificently versatile but they prove very intolerant if cooked improperly. Remember to cook rice in plenty of boiling salted water for the times specified; boil pasta in boiling salted water until 'al dente', adding just a teaspoon of oil if liked to prevent sticking; and make pancakes in heavy-based crêpe, omelette or frying pans carefully prepared to prevent them from sticking. Drain, refresh or stack according to the recipe instructions for perfect results every time.

Chicken, Walnut and Lemon Pancakes (page 76), Potato Pancakes with Green Goddess Sauce (page 81)

DEEP-FRIED RAVIOLI POCKETS

Preparation time: 40-45 minutes, plus chilling
Cooking time: 30-40 minutes

Pasta:
225 g (8 oz) plain flour
2 large eggs
2 teaspoons oil
½ teaspoon salt
water

Provençal sauce:
1 tablespoon olive oil
1 onion, peeled and finely chopped
1 garlic clove, peeled and crushed
350 g (12 oz) tomatoes, peeled, seeded and chopped
1 teaspoon dried oregano
150 ml (¼ pint) dry white wine
1 tablespoon chopped fresh parsley
1 tablespoon chopped fresh basil
dash of Tabasco sauce
2 tablespoons tomato purée
4 tablespoons double cream

Filling:
100 g (4 oz) full fat soft cheese
75 g (3 oz) chopped cooked spinach
2 tablespoons grated Parmesan cheese
¼ teaspoon ground nutmeg
oil for deep frying

1. Sift the flour on to a work surface and make a well in the centre. Place the eggs, oil and salt in the well. Mix together with the fingertips, gradually drawing the flour into the centre, adding a little water if necessary, to make a smooth elastic dough. Knead for 5-10 minutes until smooth and free from cracks. Wrap in cling film and chill for 1 hour.

2. To make the sauce, heat the oil in a pan. Add the onion and garlic and cook for about 5 minutes, until softened. Add the tomatoes, and oregano and wine and bring to the boil. Cover, reduce the heat and simmer for 15-20 minutes. Stir in the parsley, basil, Tabasco, tomato purée and salt and pepper to taste. Cook, uncovered, over a high heat for 2 minutes.

3. Meanwhile, mix the soft cheese with the spinach, Parmesan cheese and nutmeg. Prepare the sauce by puréeing the provençal sauce with the cream in a blender until smooth.

4. Roll out the pasta dough on a lightly floured surface until very thin. Cut the dough into 2 equal pieces. Spoon 12 portions of filling on to one piece, 5 cm (2 inches) apart. Using a pastry brush, dampen the dough between the mounds of stuffing. Cover the first piece of dough with the second. With the fingertips press round the dough squares so that the 2 layers stick together. When the layers are stuck, take a pastry wheel, and trim and cut out the ravioli squares.

5. Heat the oil to 180°-190°C (350°-375°F) or until a cube of bread browns in 30 seconds. Deep-fry the ravioli, a few at a time, for about 4-6 minutes until golden and cooked. Drain on paper towels.

6. Meanwhile, gently heat the sauce until hot but not boiling. Serve with the ravioli.

SAVOURY PANCAKES

Preparation time: 20 minutes
Cooking time: about 40 minutes
Oven: 190°C, 375°F, Gas Mark 5

Pancake batter:
100 g (4 oz) plain flour
1 egg
300 ml (½ pint) milk
1 tablespoon oil
pinch of salt
pinch of dried mixed herbs
Filling:
100 g (4 oz) back bacon, rinded and chopped
50 g (2 oz) flaked almonds
100 g (4 oz) mushrooms, chopped
25 g (1 oz) butter
25 g (1 oz) plain flour
300 ml (½ pint) milk
75 g (3 oz) Cheddar cheese, grated
pinch of mustard powder
freshly ground black pepper
To garnish:
8 bacon rolls, grilled until crisp
sprigs of fresh parsley

1. Place the batter ingredients in a blender goblet and blend together.
2. Use the batter to make 8 pancakes (see page 76). **F**
3. Cook the bacon in a pan without additional fat, until crisp. Add the almonds and cook until golden. Add the mushrooms and cook until softened.
4. Melt the butter in a pan. Add the flour and cook for 1 minute. Gradually add the milk, blending well. Bring to the boil and cook for 2-3 minutes, stirring constantly. Stir in the cheese until melted, then add mustard and pepper to taste. Fold in the bacon mixture, blending well.
5. Fill each pancake with an equal quantity of this filling and roll up. Place in a greased ovenproof dish. Cover with foil and bake in a preheated moderately hot oven for 20 minutes until heated through.
6. Serve hot, garnished with bacon rolls and parsley.

F Freeze pancakes, interleaved with foil or greaseproof paper, for up to 4 months. Allow to thaw in their wrappings for about 1-2 hours at room temperature.

From the top: Savoury Pancakes, Deep-Fried Ravioli Pockets

From the left: Zitone Pesaro Style, Spaghetti with Olives, Spaghetti alla Carbonara

ZITONE PESARO STYLE

Preparation time: 20 minutes
Cooking time: 50-60 minutes
Oven: 200°C, 400°F, Gas Mark 6

175 g (6 oz) turkey breast meat
2 chicken livers
100 g (4 oz) ham
50 g (2 oz) mushrooms
100 g (4 oz) butter
1 small onion, peeled and chopped
7 tablespoons dry white wine
pinch of grated nutmeg
salt
freshly ground black pepper
7 tablespoons cream
300 g (11 oz) zitone
75 g (3 oz) Gruyère cheese, grated

This recipe for cooking the extra-large macaroni which are called zitone in Italy, comes from the town of Pesaro in the Adriatic province of Marche.

1. Mince the turkey, chicken livers, ham and mushrooms. Melt 2 tablespoons butter in a heavy pan, add the onion and fry gently until golden. Stir in the minced mixture and cook, stirring, for 10 minutes.

2. Add the wine and simmer gently until it has evaporated by half, then add the nutmeg and salt and pepper to taste. Transfer to a bowl, add a little of the cream and stir well, to give a smooth, creamy filling.

3. Cook the zitone in plenty of boiling salted water until *al dente*. Drain thoroughly, then stuff with the filling.

4. Arrange the stuffed zitone in two layers in a buttered baking dish, covering each layer with the cream and Gruyère. Dot the remaining butter over the top. Bake in a preheated oven for 15 minutes. Serve hot.

SPAGHETTI ALLA CARBONARA

Preparation time: 10 minutes
Cooking time: 10-20 minutes

25 g (1 oz) butter
100 g (4 oz) bacon, diced
1 garlic clove, peeled
400 g (14 oz) spaghetti
salt
freshly ground black pepper
3 eggs, beaten
40 g (1½ oz) Parmesan cheese, grated
40 g (1½ oz) pecorino cheese, grated

1. Melt the butter in a heavy pan, add the bacon and garlic, fry gently until browned, then remove the garlic from the pan.
2. Cook the spaghetti in plenty of boiling salted water until *al dente*. Drain thoroughly and add to the bacon. Stir well, then remove from the heat.
3. Add the eggs, a pinch of pepper, half the Parmesan and half the pecorino. Toss until the eggs turn creamy yellow, then add the remaining cheeses. Toss again and serve immediately.

SPAGHETTI WITH OLIVES

Preparation time: 15 minutes
Cooking time: 25-30 minutes

150 ml (¼ pint) olive oil
1 yellow or green pepper, cored, seeded and sliced
3 tomatoes, skinned and chopped
salt
freshly ground black pepper
100 g (4 oz) black olives, halved and stoned
400 g (14 oz) spaghetti
65 g (2½ oz) pecorino or Parmesan cheese, grated

1. Heat the oil in a heavy pan, add the pepper, tomatoes and salt and pepper to taste. Cover and simmer gently for 20 minutes, stirring occasionally. Add the olives and cook for 5 minutes.
2. Meanwhile, cook the spaghetti in plenty of boiling salted water until *al dente*. Drain thoroughly and add to the sauce. Fold gently to mix, then pile into a warmed serving dish and sprinkle with the cheese. Serve immediately.

CHICKEN, WALNUT AND LEMON PANCAKES

Preparation time: 10 minutes
Cooking time: 40 minutes
Oven: 190°C, 375°F, Gas Mark 4

Pancake batter:
100 g (4 oz) plain flour
1 egg
300 ml (½ pint) milk
1 tablespoon oil
pinch of salt
oil for cooking
Filling:
25 g (1 oz) butter
25 g (1 oz) plain flour
300 ml (½ pint) milk
finely grated rind of 1 lemon
225 g (8 oz) cooked chicken, chopped
40 g (1½ oz) walnuts, coarsely chopped
salt and black pepper
1 tablespoon lemon juice
chopped walnuts, to garnish

1. Place the batter ingredients in a blender goblet and blend together. Heat a little oil in a small crêpe or omelette pan. Pour in about 2 tablespoons of the batter. Cook on each side until the pancake is golden. Stack between greaseproof paper. This batter will make 8 pancakes.
2. For the filling, melt the butter in a pan. Add the flour and cook for 1 minute. Gradually add the milk, blending well. Bring to the boil and cook for 2-3 minutes, stirring constantly. Remove 4 tablespoons of the sauce and set aside.
3. Add the lemon rind, chicken, walnuts and salt and pepper to taste to the sauce, blending well.
4. Fill each pancake with an equal quantity of this filling and roll up. Place in a greased ovenproof dish. Mix the reserved sauce with the lemon juice and salt and pepper to taste and spoon over the pancakes. Cover with foil and bake for 20 minutes.
5. Serve hot sprinkled with walnuts.

Illustrated on page 70

CRÊPES AUX FRUITS DE MER

Preparation time: 20 minutes
Cooking time: 40-45 minutes, including making pancakes
Oven: 200°C, 400°F, Gas Mark 6

300 ml (½ pint) crêpe (pancake) batter (see above)
225 g (8 oz) haddock or cod, skinned and boned
150 ml (¼ pint) white wine
4 scallops
50 g (2 oz) butter, plus extra for greasing
1 medium onion, peeled and finely chopped
100 g (4 oz) button mushrooms, thinly sliced
1 teaspoon lemon juice
salt
white pepper
25 g (1 oz) plain flour
about 150 ml (¼ pint) milk
4 tablespoons double or whipping cream
100 g (4 oz) peeled prawns
4 tablespoons grated Gruyère cheese
8 whole prawns, to garnish

1. Make 4 large pancakes or 8 smaller ones and keep hot (see recipe above).
2. Poach the haddock in the white wine over a gentle heat for 10-12 minutes.
3. Cut the scallops into 4 and add to the pan. Cook for a further 2-3 minutes. Drain, reserving the liquor. Flake the haddock and reserve.
4. Meanwhile, melt 25 g (1 oz) of the butter in a pan, add the onion and cook gently until soft but not coloured.
5. Melt the remaining butter in another pan and add the mushrooms, lemon juice, salt and pepper. Cover and cook for a few minutes until soft.
6. When the onions are soft, add the flour. Cook for 1-2 minutes, stirring, then add the fish cooking liquor and milk. Bring to the boil and cook for 2-3 minutes, stirring.
7. Add the cream, haddock, scallops, mushrooms and prawns. Reheat, and thin the sauce if necessary with a little milk.
8. Place some of the mixture on each pancake. Roll up and place in a buttered ovenproof dish. Sprinkle the cheese over.
9. Place in a preheated oven and cook for 7-10 minutes or under a preheated hot grill to allow the cheese to melt.
10. Serve hot, garnished with prawns.

Crêpes aux Fruits de Mer

FLAMED TAGLIATELLE WITH YOGURT

Preparation time: 10 minutes
Cooking time: 10 minutes

350 g (12 oz) wholewheat tagliatelle, or
other pasta shapes
salt
50 g (2 oz) butter
3 tablespoons brandy
150 ml (¼ pint) plain unsweetened yogurt
60 g (2½ oz) grated Parmesan cheese
freshly ground black pepper
50 g (2 oz) walnut halves, to garnish

1. Cook the tagliatelle in plenty of boiling, salted water for about 10 minutes, or according to the directions on the packet, until it is just tender. Drain, refresh in hot water, and drain again.
2. Melt the butter in a pan and toss the tagliatelle to coat thoroughly. Pour on the brandy, stir well and light it, to burn off the alcohol.
3. Stir in the yogurt and cheese, and season with plenty of black pepper. Garnish with the walnuts and serve at once.

CANNELLONI WITH SPINACH FILLING

Preparation time: 50 minutes
Cooking time: 1 hour
Oven: 180°C, 350°F, Gas Mark 4
Serves 4-6

750 g (1½ lb) fresh spinach, stalks removed
50 g (2 oz) butter
225 g (8 oz) Ricotta or cottage cheese,
sieved
75 g (3 oz) grated Parmesan cheese
salt
freshly ground black pepper
pinch of grated nutmeg
2 large eggs
12 large cannelloni tubes
25 g (1 oz) flour
300 ml (½ pint) milk
4 tablespoons bran cereal

1. Wash the spinach and cook in the water clinging to the leaves in a large pan for 12 minutes over moderate heat. Stir frequently. Drain the spinach in a colander, pressing out all moisture. Chop the spinach finely.
2. Melt half the butter in a pan, add the spinach and stir well. Remove from the heat.
3. Beat the sieved Ricotta or cottage cheese and half the Parmesan cheese into the spinach and season with salt, pepper and nutmeg. Beat in the eggs. Set aside to cool.
4. Cook the cannelloni tubes in plenty of boiling, salted water for about 10 minutes, or according to the direction of the packet, until they are just tender. Drain, refresh in cold water, and drain again. Dry thoroughly with kitchen paper. Set aside to cool.
5. Melt the remaining butter in a pan, stir in the flour, and cook for 1 minute. Remove from the heat and gradually stir in the milk, stirring constantly. Bring to the boil, season with salt and pepper and simmer for 5 minutes. Taste and adjust the seasoning if necessary.
6. Use a piping bag (but no nozzle) to fill the cannelloni tubes with the spinach mixture.
7. Place the filled cannelloni in a greased, shallow baking dish. Pour over the sauce and sprinkle with the remaining cheese mixed with the cereal.
8. Bake on a baking sheet in a preheated oven for 35-40 minutes, or until the topping is brown and crusty.

CARAMELLI WITH BASIL SAUCE

Preparation time: 15 minutes
Cooking time: 12 minutes

350 g (12 oz) wholewheat caramelli shells,
or other pasta shapes
salt
75 g (3 oz) fresh basil leaves
4 tablespoons olive oil
3 garlic cloves, peeled and crushed
50 g (2 oz) pine kernels, or blanched
slivered almonds
50 g (2 oz) grated Parmesan cheese
25 g (1 oz) softened butter
freshly ground black pepper

This sauce, made with fresh basil leaves, is known as pesto, and originated in Genoa. You can grow basil during the summer in a greenhouse or on a sunny windowsill. However, if you do not have a plentiful supply, experiment with other herbs. Both marjoram and mint make interesting substitutes.
1. Cook the pasta in plenty of boiling, salted water for about 12 minutes, or according to the directions on the packet, until it is just tender. Drain, refresh in hot water and drain again, tossing to ensure that no water is trapped inside. Keep hot.
2. To make the sauce, liquidize the herb leaves, oil, garlic and nuts in a blender. Scrape out the mixture, beat in the cheese and butter and season with pepper.
3. Spoon the sauce over the hot pasta and serve at once, as an accompaniment to meat and poultry, or on its own.

Clockwise from top right: Flamed Tagliatelle with Yogurt, Caramelli with Basil Sauce, Cannelloni with Spinach Filling

RISOTTO WITH SCAMPI

Preparation time: 25 minutes
Cooking time: 40-45 minutes
Serves 4-6

450 g (1 lb) fresh scampi
1 litre (1¾ pints) water
1 bay leaf, chopped
2 garlic cloves, peeled and chopped
salt
3 tablespoons olive oil
75 g (3 oz) butter, softened
1 onion, peeled and chopped
400 g (14 oz) rice
3-4 tablespoons white wine
freshly ground black pepper

If fresh scampi is unobtainable, thawed frozen scampi may be used instead. Omit the first stage of precooking the scampi in seasoned water and use a fish stock or light chicken stock as the cooking liquor for the risotto.

1. Wash the scampi and put them in a pan with the water, bay leaf, garlic and a pinch of salt. Bring to the boil and cook for 5 minutes. Remove the scampi from the water with a slotted spoon and peel off the shells. Return the shells to the water and boil for a further 5 minutes, then strain and keep the stock hot.

2. Meanwhile, dice the scampi. Heat the oil and 2 tablespoons butter in a large heavy pan, add the onion and fry gently until golden. Stir in the rice, then add the wine. Cook gently for 15 minutes, stirring frequently. Add the stock a little at a time to moisten as necessary during cooking.

3. Add the scampi, remaining butter and salt and pepper to taste, then cook for a further 5 to 10 minutes until the rice is just tender. Remove from the heat, leave to stand for 1 minute, then serve.

CHICKEN RISOTTO

Preparation time: 30 minutes
Cooking time: about 2 hours
Serves 6-8

1 × 1 kg (2-2½ lb) oven-ready chicken
2 litres (3½ pints) water
2 celery sticks
2 onions, peeled
2 carrots, peeled
salt
freshly ground black pepper
3-4 tablespoons olive oil
7 tablespoons white wine
350 g (12 oz) tomatoes, skinned and mashed
450 g (1 lb) rice
75 g (3 oz) butter, softened
75 g (3 oz) Parmesan cheese, grated

1. Remove the bones from the chicken and place them in a large pan with the water. Add 1 celery stick, 1 onion and 1 carrot and season with salt and pepper. Bring to the boil, lower the heat, cover and simmer for 1½ hours. Strain the stock and keep hot.

2. Meanwhile, dice the chicken meat, removing all skin. Finely chop the remaining vegetables. Heat the oil in a large heavy pan, add the vegetables and fry gently until lightly coloured. Add the chicken and fry for a further 5 minutes, stirring constantly, then add the wine and boil until it evaporates.

3. Add the tomatoes and salt and pepper to taste. Cover and cook gently for 20 minutes, adding a little of the chicken stock if the mixture becomes dry.

4. Stir in the rice, then add 200 ml (⅓ pint) chicken stock. Cook for 20 to 25 minutes until the rice is just tender, adding a little more stock to moisten, as necessary.

5. Remove from the heat, add the butter and Parmesan and fold gently to mix. Serve immediately.

POTATO PANCAKES WITH GREEN GODDESS SAUCE

Preparation time: 15 minutes
Cooking time: 10 minutes

6 medium potatoes, peeled and grated
2 eggs
1½ teaspoons salt
¼ teaspoon freshly ground black pepper
¼ teaspoon ground paprika
1 small onion, peeled and grated
pinch of ground mace
1 tablespoon plain flour
oil for shallow frying
Sauce:
250 ml (8 fl oz) mayonnaise
1 teaspoon anchovy essence
3 spring onions, finely chopped
2 tablespoons chopped parsley
2 teaspoons chopped tarragon
1 tablespoon tarragon vinegar
freshly ground black pepper
150 ml (¼ pint) soured cream

Illustrated on page 70

1. Rinse the potatoes and pat dry with absorbent kitchen paper. Beat the eggs with the salt, pepper, paprika, onion, mace and flour, blending well. Stir in the grated potato.
2. Divide the mixture into 8 equal portions. Shallow fry the potato pancakes in two batches, in hot oil in a frying pan, flattening each slightly with a spatula. Fry slowly, turning once, for about 5 minutes until crisp, golden and cooked through. Drain on absorbent kitchen paper and keep warm while cooking the second batch.
3. Meanwhile to make the sauce, mix the mayonnaise with the anchovy essence, spring onions, parsley, tarragon, vinegar and pepper to taste, blending well. Fold in the soured cream and chill until required.
4. Serve the warm pancakes with the chilled sauce.

From the left: *Chicken Risotto, Risotto with Scampi*

TRIFLES, FOOLS & MOUSSES

**Deliciously fruity or liquor-soaked; rich and creamy or
light and refreshing; fluffy and wispy – all these
descriptions can apply to trifles, fools and mousses.**

Rich in their use of fruit, cream, eggs, sponge and juice or
liquor flavourings these dishes can take on a different guise
almost every time they are made. No one could deny the
wealth of differences between a light berry-filled trifle for
summertime eating and the festive Christmas affair laden with
dried or flown-in foreign fruits, lashings of cream and more
than a splash or two of brandy, port, sherry or rum. Compare
the similarities, or lack of them, between a rich thick mousse
for chocoholics and a light and fluffy yet piquant grapefruit
mousse and you can see, within this repertoire, there are the
makings for some deliciously different endings to fine meals
for all occasions.

Most are made using more than a little cream, often a few
eggs and some other flavouring ingredient of a pleasurable
nature, so they are rarely the desserts to choose for the avid
slimmer or the faint-hearted. If choosing them, opt for starters
and main courses that do not include eggs, cream or alcohol or
the whole menu could prove heavy and unbalanced. Ideal
starters are light vegetable-based soups, marinated raw fish
dishes, simple grilled seafood and appetising vegetable and
fruit salads, while main courses could include a simple roast
rack of lamb served with redcurrant jelly, chicken casseroled in
stock with fresh vegetables and chopped herb garnish, or
baked whole fish like grey mullet served with a piquant
cucumber salad.

After such careful restraint, trifle, fool and mousse desserts
can then be decorated with wickedly delicious accompaniments like chocolate leaves or rose petals, sweetened crème
chantilly, crushed almond praline, dainty sweet biscuits,
chopped nuts or simple whipped cream. When there is time to
spare, pipe the cream lavishly in swirls and rosettes for a truly
spectacular dessert.

*From the top: Mocca
Soufflé (page 87),
Grapefruit Mousse (page
88)*

Chocolate Mousse

CHOCOLATE MOUSSE

Preparation time: 25 minutes, plus setting
Serves 4-6

225 g (8 oz) plain chocolate
25 g (1 oz) unsalted butter
3 eggs, separated
2 tablespoons whisky
1 egg white

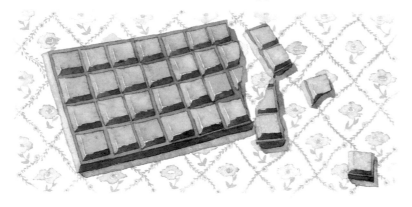

1. Break the chocolate into small pieces and place in a heatproof bowl with the butter. Stand over a pan of simmering water until the chocolate has melted.
2. Put 2 teaspoons of melted chocolate on to a piece of greaseproof paper and spread thinly with a palette knife. Leave to set. Beat the egg yolks and whisky into the bowl of chocolate and chill until cool, but do not allow the mixture to set.
3. Whisk all 4 egg whites in a bowl until stiff and fold into the chocolate mixture.
4. Pour into four 150 ml (¼ pint) ramekin dishes or six 100 ml (4 fl oz) chocolate pots. Ⓐ Ⓕ Chill for at least 6 hours until set. Cut the melted chocolate into triangles and decorate the mousses.

Ⓐ Can be prepared the day before and stored in the refrigerator.
Ⓕ Cover and freeze for up to 6 months. Thaw in the refrigerator for 4-5 hours.

RASPBERRY TRIFLES

Preparation time: 30 minutes, plus standing
and chilling
Cooking time: 5 minutes

65 g (2½ oz) sugar
50 ml (2 fl oz) water
25 ml (1 fl oz) raspberry liqueur or Kirsch
20 sponge fingers
4 ratafias
4 heaped teaspoons raspberry jam
fresh raspberries, to decorate
Crème Anglaise:
3 egg yolks
60 g (2¼ oz) vanilla sugar
250 ml (8 fl oz) full cream milk
Crème Chantilly:
150 ml (5 fl oz) double cream
25 ml (1 fl oz) egg white
25 g (1 oz) caster or vanilla sugar

1. Boil the sugar and water in a heavy-based saucepan until the sugar dissolves. Cool, then add the liqueur or Kirsch.
2. Break the sponge fingers into several pieces and arrange in a bowl with the ratafias. Pour over the syrup.
3. Spoon half the sponge fingers into the bottoms of 4 glass dishes. Spoon the raspberry jam over the top and cover with the remaining biscuits and ratafias.
4. To make the crème Anglaise whisk the yolks and sugar until creamy. Gently heat the milk to simmering point, then pour it over the egg yolk mixture.
5. Pour into the rinsed pan. Heat gently, stirring continuously, until the sauce coats the back of a wooden spoon. Take care as it will curdle if it is boiled.
6. Pour the crème Anglaise into the 4 glass dishes. Cool for 15 minutes then chill.
7. Prepare the crème Chantilly. Put the cream in a mixing bowl, add the egg white and whisk until the cream holds its shape on the whisk. Add the sugar. Whisk until the cream is smooth and holds its shape.
8. Fit a piping bag with a large star nozzle and fill with the crème Chantilly. Decorate the top edge of the 4 trifles with rosettes of cream and top each one with a raspberry.

Raspberry Trifles

MARBLED GOOSEBERRY FOOL

Preparation time: 12 minutes, plus cooling and chilling
Cooking time: about 30 minutes
Serves 5-6

750 g (1½ lb) fresh or frozen and thawed
gooseberries, topped and tailed
175 g (6 oz) caster sugar
1 teaspoon powdered gelatine
2 tablespoons water
150 ml (¼ pint) whipping cream
1 × 425 g (15 oz) can custard
a few drops green food colouring
(optional)

1. Put the gooseberries and sugar in a pan and heat gently until the sugar has dissolved. Simmer, uncovered, until the fruit forms a thick pulp. Stir the mixture occasionally to prevent it sticking.
2. Purée the mixture in a blender or food processor then sieve to remove the seeds. Leave the mixture to cool for about 30 minutes.
3. Meanwhile, sprinkle the gelatine over the water in a heatproof basin and leave to soften for 5 minutes. Stand the basin in a pan of gently simmering water and leave until the gelatine has dissolved.
4. Whip the cream until it forms soft peaks and stir in the cooled, but still liquid gelatine. Lightly whisk in the custard.
5. Tint the cooled gooseberry purée with a few drops of green colouring, if liked. Put alternate spoonfuls of the gooseberry purée and custard mixture into individual glasses, finishing with the custard.
6. Pull the handle of a teaspoon from the top to the base at 2.5 cm (1 inch) intervals around the inside of each glass to create a 'marbled' effect. Chill for at least 1 hour before serving.

From left: Caramel Party Mousse (page 89), Marbled Gooseberry Fool

MOCHA SOUFFLÉ

Preparation time: 30 minutes, plus cooling and setting
Cooking time: 6-8 minutes
Serves 6-8

3 teaspoons instant coffee granules
3 tablespoons boiling water
3 teaspoons powdered gelatine
100 g (4 oz) plain chocolate, broken in pieces
5 eggs, separated
150 g (5 oz) caster sugar
300 ml (½ pint) double cream
To decorate:
25 g (1 oz) chocolate vermicelli
150 ml (¼ pint) whipping cream
crystallised rose petals

1. Prepare the soufflé dish: tie a band of double thickness greaseproof paper or foil around the outside of a 15 cm (6 inch) diameter/1.2 litres (2 pint) capacity soufflé dish, to stand at least 5 cm (2 inches) above the rim of the dish.
2. Dissolve the coffee in the boiling water in a heatproof bowl and leave to cool. Sprinkle the gelatine over the coffee and leave to soften for 5 minutes. Stand the bowl in a pan of simmering water and leave until the gelatine dissolves. Leave to cool, but not set. Meanwhile, put the pieces of chocolate into a heatproof bowl standing over a pan of simmering water and leave to melt.
3. Now, put the egg yolks and sugar in a heatproof bowl set over a saucepan of very hot water, off the heat. Whisk for about 3 minutes, with an electric hand-held whisk until creamy, thick and pale. Remove from the heat and whisk in the melted chocolate. Whisk the mixture again until cold.
4. Whisk in the cooled, runny gelatine mixture until evenly combined. Leave the mixture in the refrigerator for 5-10 minutes, or until just beginning to set around the edges.
5. Whisk the egg whites stiffly; whisk the cream until softly peaking. Gently fold the egg whites and the cream into the chocolate mixture, using a large metal spoon.
6. Turn the mixture into the prepared soufflé dish and smooth the surface. Leave to set in a cool place for several hours or overnight.
7. Carefully peel away the greaseproof paper or foil, using a knife to help. Coat the exposed sides of the soufflé with chocolate vermicelli. Decorate the top with 8 swirls of whipped cream and place rose petals between them.

Illustrated on page 82

VICTORIA SYLLABUB

Preparation time: 10 minutes

300 ml (½ pint) double cream
65 g (2½ oz) caster sugar
1 lemon
50 ml (2 fl oz) Madeira
julienne of lemon rind, to decorate

1. Whip the double cream and sugar until it holds its shape on the whisk.
2. Grate the rind of half the lemon then squeeze the juice from the whole fruit. Combine with the Madeira.
3. Whisk the rind, juice and Madeira into the cream, a little at a time, until the syllabub holds its shape on the whisk. Spoon into 4 wine glasses. Decorate with the julienne and serve accompanied by biscuits such as brandysnaps.

RHUBARB FOOL

Preparation time: 20 minutes, plus cooling and chilling
Cooking time: approx. 10 minutes

200 g (7 oz) rhubarb, chopped into 2.5 cm (1 inch) lengths
40 g (1½ oz) caster sugar
40 g (1½ oz) clear honey
300 ml (½ pint) double cream

Try making this fool with other fruits. Firm fruits would need to be liquidized after stewing. Fruits with seeds can be strained through a sieve after stewing, if liked, to remove the seeds.
1. Place the rhubarb in a pan with a tablespoon of water. Cover and stew till tender. Add the sugar and honey, then leave to cool.
2. Whip the cream until it holds its shape on the whisk. Beat the rhubarb and juice into the cream a little at a time, then spoon into 4 wine glasses and chill.

GRAPEFRUIT MOUSSE

Preparation time: 25 minutes, plus setting time
Cooking time: 3 minutes
Serves 6

4 eggs, separated
100 g (4 oz) caster sugar
3 tablespoons cold water
3 teaspoons powdered gelatine
finely grated rind 1 grapefruit
150 ml (¼ pint) freshly squeezed grapefruit juice
To decorate:
shredded grapefruit rind
sprigs of fresh mint

Illustrated on page 82

1. Whisk egg yolks and sugar in a bowl until the mixture is light and fluffy.
2. Put the water into a heatproof bowl. Sprinkle the gelatine over the water and leave to soften for 5 minutes. Stand the bowl in a pan of gently simmering water and leave until the gelatine dissolves. Remove from the heat. Stir in the grapefruit rind and juice. Stir well and leave to cool, but not set.
3. Add the gelatine mixture in a thin steady stream to the whisked egg and sugar mixture, whisking well all the time. Leave the mixture in the refrigerator for about 10 minutes or until it is just beginning to set around the edges.
4. Stiffly whisk the egg whites and, using a metal spoon, lightly fold into the grapefruit mixture. Whisk very lightly for a few seconds to give a smooth mixture.
5. Spoon the mixture into individual glass dishes and leave to set for several hours.
6. Decorate with grapefruit rind and mint.

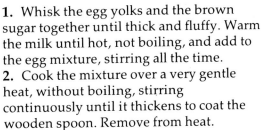

CARAMEL PARTY MOUSSE

Preparation time: 20-30 minutes, plus cooling and chilling
Cooking time: 15 minutes
Serves 6-8

4 egg yolks
50 g (2 oz) soft light brown sugar
600 ml (1 pint) milk
225 g (8 oz) granulated sugar
175 ml (6 fl oz) cold water
1 × 11 g (0.4 oz) packet gelatine
3 tablespoons orange juice
150 ml (¼ pint) whipping cream
2 egg whites
Almond praline:
120 g (4½ oz) unblanched almonds
100 g (4 oz) caster sugar
150-300 ml (¼-½ pint) double cream, to decorate

Illustrated on pages 86-7

1. Whisk the egg yolks and the brown sugar together until thick and fluffy. Warm the milk until hot, not boiling, and add to the egg mixture, stirring all the time.
2. Cook the mixture over a very gentle heat, without boiling, stirring continuously until it thickens to coat the wooden spoon. Remove from heat.
3. Dissolve the granulated sugar in 85 ml (3 fl oz) of the water in a pan, bring to the boil and boil rapidly until turned golden. Remove from the heat and holding the pan with a cloth, slowly add the remaining cold water. Heat gently, stirring, to dissolve the caramel. Remove from the heat and slowly add to the custard.
4. Sprinkle the gelatine over the orange juice in a heatproof basin and leave to soften for 5 minutes. Stand the basin in a pan of gently simmering water and leave until the gelatine has dissolved.
5. Stir the cooled gelatine into the custard; chill until beginning to set at the edges.
6. Whip the cream until it forms peaks; stiffly whisk the egg whites. Lightly fold both into the mixture. Turn into a serving dish and set in the refrigerator.
7. To make the praline, put the almonds and sugar in a non-stick frying pan. Heat very gently until the sugar melts and cooks to a rich dark golden brown. Pour on to a well-greased baking sheet and leave to set.
8. Just before serving decorate with cream and the crushed praline.

From the left: Victoria Syllabub, Rhubarb Fool

LORD MAYOR'S TRIFLE

Preparation time: 40 minutes, plus soaking
Cooking time: 15 minutes
Serves 8

6 sponge cakes, about 10 × 5 cm (4 × 2 inches)
1 packet (approx. 40) small ratafia biscuits
8 small almond macaroons
150 ml (¼ pint) brandy or sherry
Custard:
600 ml (1 pint) milk
2 tablespoons caster sugar
4 egg yolks, beaten
To finish:
6 tablespoons strawberry or raspberry jam
300 ml (½ pint) double or whipping cream, whipped
2 tablespoons flaked toasted almonds, to decorate

1. Slice the sponge cakes and put at the bottom of a deep dish. Reserving half the ratafia biscuits, add the rest and the macaroons, crumbled. Pour over the brandy or sherry and leave, covered, to soak for at least 4 hours.
2. To make the custard heat the milk with the sugar until the sugar has dissolved. Pour the milk over the egg yolks, beating all the time.
3. Return to the saucepan, and stir over a moderate heat until the liquid will coat the back of a spoon. Do not allow the custard to boil or it will curdle.
4. Remove from the heat and stir to prevent a skin forming. Allow to cool, covered.
5. Spread the jam over the sponge cakes.
6. Pour the cold custard over the cakes.
7. About 30 minutes before serving, cover the top with the whipped cream piled high, and decorate with the reserved ratafia biscuits and toasted almonds.

CREAMY BLACKBERRY FOOL

Preparation time: 12 minutes, plus cooling and chilling
Cooking time: 15 minutes
Serves 6

450 g (1 lb) fresh or frozen (thawed) blackberries
100 g (4 oz) caster sugar
25 g (1 oz) butter
300 ml (½ pint) whipping cream
1 large jam-filled Swiss roll, sliced (optional)

From the top: *Lord Mayor's Trifle, Creamy Blackberry Fool*

1. Put the blackberries into a saucepan with the sugar and butter. Cover and cook over a gentle heat for about 15 minutes until the blackberries are tender. Remove from the heat and allow to cool slightly.
2. Pass the contents of the pan through a sieve into a bowl, pressing well with the back of a wooden spoon to extract as much juice and pulp as possible; discard all the seeds. Leave to cool completely. **A**
3. Whip the cream until stiff, reserve 2 tablespoons for decoration, and gently fold in the strained blackberry syrup, using a spatula to mix until evenly blended.
4. Place slices of Swiss roll in a glass serving dish, if using, and spoon the blackberry mixture on top.
5. To finish, pipe parallel lines of the reserved cream across the fool and draw a cocktail stick across in alternate directions to give a feathered effect.
6. Chill in the refrigerator for at least one hour before serving.

A The blackberry purée can be prepared several hours in advance.

PIES, FLANS & PASTRIES

If you are a competent pastrycook then you have the makings of some splendid and unforgettable pies, flans and pastries literally at your fingertips.

Few puddings and desserts are greeted with such enthusiasm as the sugar-glazed and golden-crusted home-baked and fruit-filled pie, the delicately moulded and arranged continental tart and seemingly endlessly layered flaky strudel. Such is the wonderful reception, it is the wise cook who makes the pastry concoction the masterpiece of her dessert repertoire.

Apart from the familiar shortcrust, flan or sweet crisp pastry, there are many other pastry types and pastry alternatives to experiment with. Try lusciously cream-filled flaky pastry slices dusted liberally with sifted icing sugar or a crunchy no-bake digestive biscuit crust for a fluffy pinky marshmallow filling, for example. If pressed for time, then look at the vast array of ready-made shortcrust, flaky and strudel pastries on offer all ready for rolling. They come in many varieties and sizes from plain to wholemeal to block, ready-rolled sheets and ready-shaped tartlets for pure convenience.

Whatever your choice, remember to treat pastry with respect. Keep utensils and hands as cool as possible during preparation, roll out the pastry with care, trying not to overstretch, allow it to rest in the refrigerator for the times specified and bake at the correct temperature until crisp and golden.

Needless to say, if your pudding or dessert is of the pastry kind avoid the same for a starter or main course. Ideal starters to serve before what are often substantial dessert pastries include vegetable crudités served with a selection of dips, stuffed mushrooms or tomatoes, steamed mussels or a light vegetable consommé. Aim to serve equally light and refreshing main courses, too: goujons of sole served with a tartare sauce, perhaps, or a fragrant fish-filled pilaf, paella or risotto or small portion of veal olives. Serve them with a crisp seasonal salad or colourful array of boiled or steamed vegetables to ensure the appetite is not overloaded before the crispy pastry treat to come.

From the top: Rhubarb Crumble Flan (page 102), French Apple Tartlets (page 102), Apple Strudel (page 98)

Glazed Gooseberry Boats

GLAZED GOOSEBERRY BOATS

Preparation time: 40 minutes, plus cooling
Cooking time: 45 minutes
Oven: 180°C, 350°F, Gas Mark 4; then 150°C,
300°F, Gas Mark 2
Serves 6

Pastry:
150 g (5 oz) plain flour, sifted
75 g (3 oz) butter, cut into small chunks
50 g (2 oz) caster sugar
2 egg yolks
Filling:
225 g (8 oz) gooseberries, topped and tailed
75 g (3 oz) sugar
4 tablespoons water
Glaze:
4 tablespoons apricot jam, sieved
2 tablespoons water
1 × 150 ml (5 fl oz) carton double or
whipping cream, whipped, to decorate

1. Make the pastry. Place the flour on a board or marble slab, and make a well in the centre. Put the butter, caster sugar and egg yolks into the well, then gradually work all the ingredients together until they form a stiff dough. Knead gently until smooth.

2. To make the boats, roll out the pastry and use it to line 12 boat-shaped pastry moulds.

3. Prick the bases of the pastry and bake in a preheated oven for 8-10 minutes, or until the pastry is crisp, and golden brown around the edges.

4. Remove the pastry boats from the tins, and allow them to cool on a wire tray.

5. Place the gooseberries in an oven-proof dish, sprinkle with the sugar, then pour over the water. Cook in a preheated cool oven until the fruit is just tender. The cooking time depends on the ripeness of the gooseberries, but remove them from the oven before they begin to break up. Allow to cool in the dish.

6. When the gooseberries are quite cold, fill them into the pastry boats and prepare the glaze.

7. Place the apricot jam and water in a small saucepan and allow to melt over a gentle heat. Bring to simmering point and cook for 2-3 minutes. Using a pastry brush, glaze each pastry boat.

8. For the decoration, fill the whipped cream into a forcing bag fitted with a small rose tube, and pipe each boat with a shell pattern.

FLAKY CREAM SLICES

Preparation time: 15 minutes, plus resting and cooling
Cooking time: 8-10 minutes
Oven: 230°C, 450°F, Gas Mark 8
Makes 10

1 × 215 g (7½ oz) packet frozen puff pastry, thawed
150 ml (¼ pint) whipping cream
3 teaspoons icing sugar, sifted
a few drops of vanilla essence
225 g (8 oz) strawberries, hulled and halved

Illustrated on pages 96-7

Flaky layers of golden pastry, sandwiched together with fruit and cream, make a delicious menu finale.

1. Cut the pastry in half lengthways and place one strip on top of the other. Roll out the pastry on a lightly floured board or work surface to a 50 × 10 cm (20 × 4 inch) rectangle.

2. Cut the pastry crossways into 5 × 10 cm (2 × 4 inch) pieces. Place these on a dampened baking sheet and set aside for 15 minutes.

3. Bake in a preheated oven for 8-10 minutes until golden brown and cooked through. Remove from the oven, carefully transfer to a wire rack and leave to cool completely. [A]

4. Carefully split each pastry rectangle in half, to give 2 layers. In a bowl, whip the cream with 1 teaspoon of the icing sugar and vanilla essence to taste, until stiff. Spread the 10 pastry bases with whipped cream and arrange the strawberry halves on top. Add the remaining pastry layers and dredge with the remaining icing sugar.

[A] Can be prepared 5 days in advance, then stored in an airtight tin. Reheat the pastry rectangles at 180°C, 350°F, Gas Mark 4 for 5 minutes to refresh and crisp. Cool completely before splitting and filling.

Variation: If fresh strawberries are not available, replace with strawberry jam and decorate with a little reserved whipped cream.

Vary the flavour of jam: try blackberry, apricot, raspberry or black cherry.

BUTTERSCOTCH MERINGUE PIE

Preparation time: 30 minutes, plus chilling and cooling
Cooking time: 1 hour 5 minutes
Oven: 200°C, 400°F, Gas Mark 6; then 150°C, 300°F, Gas Mark 2
Serves 8-10

175 g (6 oz) soft margarine
pinch of salt
1½ tablespoons cold water
275 g (10 oz) plain flour
75 g (3 oz) butter
175 g (6 oz) soft dark brown sugar
200 ml (7 fl oz) boiling water
3 tablespoons cornflour
450 ml (¾ pint) milk
2 eggs, separated
75 g (3 oz) caster sugar

From the left:
Butterscotch Meringue Pie, Flaky Cream Slices (page 95)

1. Put the margarine with the salt, water and 2 tablespoons of the flour into a bowl and mix vigorously with a fork for 30 seconds until thoroughly blended. Add the remaining flour and continue mixing with a fork to form a fairly firm dough. Knead gently until free from cracks. Wrap in cling film and chill in the refrigerator for at least 15 minutes before using. [A]
2. Roll out the pastry on a lightly floured board or work surface to a 30 cm (12 inch) round and use to line a 25 cm (10 inch) loose-bottomed fluted flan tin, set on a baking sheet. Gently ease the pastry into the tin and press it on to the base and up the sides, pressing firmly into the flutes but taking care not to stretch the pastry. Fold the excess pastry over the edge of the tin and run a rolling pin firmly over the top to cut through the pastry and give a neat edge.
3. Prick the pastry base with a fork.

. Line with a large round of greaseproof paper or foil and fill with baking beans. Bake in a preheated oven for 15 minutes. Remove the paper and beans and return to the oven for a further 5-10 minutes until the pastry is dry and light golden-brown. Remove from the oven and leave to cool. **A** **F**

. Melt the butter in a heavy-based saucepan until just turning light golden and foaming. Add the sugar and stir well, then remove from the heat. Add the boiling water and stir well.

. Blend the cornflour with a little of the milk, to make a smooth paste. Put the remaining milk in a saucepan, and stir in the blended cornflour and the butter and sugar mixture. Place over a gentle heat and bring to the boil, stirring all the time with a wooden spoon. Lower the heat and simmer for 1 minute, stirring all the time. Remove from the heat and cool slightly.

7. Pour half the mixture on to the egg yolks in a bowl, beating well all the time, then return this to the mixture in the pan and cook over a very gentle heat for 2 minutes, stirring all the time. Remove from the heat and pour into the prepared flan case. Leave for 1 hour to cool completely. **A**

8. Whisk the egg whites until stiff, sprinkle over 40 g (1½ oz) of the sugar and whisk again until very stiff and glossy. Lightly fold in the remaining sugar, using a large metal spoon. Spoon the meringue evenly over the cold filling in the pastry case and peak, using the flat side of a knife.

9. Reduce the oven temperature and bake the flan for 30 minutes until the meringue is set and lightly browned. Leave to cool for 2 hours before serving cold, cut into slices.

A The pastry can be prepared the previous day, covered with cling film and kept chilled.

The flan case can be baked a week in advance and stored in an airtight tin, before filling.

The filled flan case can be prepared in the morning and kept at room temperature before proceeding from step 8.

F Freeze for up to 6 months. Thaw the pastry flan case for 1½ hours at room temperature before proceeding from step 5.

M Or microwave on Defrost for 2-3 minutes, then stand for 5 minutes before proceeding from step 5.

APRICOT TART

Preparation time: 35 minutes, plus resting
Cooking time: 25 minutes
Oven: 200°C, 400°F, Gas Mark 6; then 190°C,
375°F, Gas Mark 5

½ quantity Pâte sablée (see opposite)
8 large fresh apricots, halved, reserve
4 stones
150 g (5 oz) vanilla sugar
250 ml (8 fl oz) water
Crème pâtissière:
2 eggs
75 g (3 oz) vanilla sugar
25 g (1 oz) cornflour
250 ml (8 fl oz) milk

1. Line a 20 cm (8 inch) flan ring with the pastry. Rest for 30 minutes. Bake blind in preheated oven for 15 minutes. Remove the greaseproof paper and baking beans. Reduce the heat and bake for a further 10 minutes. Remove the ring and cool.
2. Crack 4 of the apricot stones and remove the kernels.
3. Put the kernels, vanilla sugar and water in a pan and simmer for 5 minutes. Add the apricots and poach for about 10 minutes until tender. Drain the apricots on absorbent kitchen paper.
4. For the Crème pâtissière, whisk the eggs and sugar together until light and creamy then whisk in the cornflour. Heat the milk to simmering point then pour over the egg and sugar mixture. Return the mixture to the rinsed pan and heat, stirring constantly, until the sauce thickens. Pour into a clean bowl, whisk briefly, then cool.
5. Spread the Crème pâtissière in to the flan and arrange the apricot halves on top.

APPLE STRUDEL

Preparation time: 35-40 minutes
Cooking time: 50 minutes
Oven: 190°C, 375°F, Gas Mark 5
Makes 2 (Serves 8)

175 g (6 oz) butter
75 g (3 oz) dry white breadcrumbs
75 g (3 oz) caster sugar
50 g (2 oz) sultanas
75 g (3 oz) toasted, blanched almonds,
coarsely chopped
¼ teaspoon ground cinnamon
freshly grated nutmeg, to taste
4 sheets filo pastry
2 large cooking apples, peeled, cored and
cut in 5 mm (¼ inch) thick slices
To finish:
1 tablespoon icing sugar

Illustrated on page 92

1. Melt 50 g (2 oz) of the butter in a frying pan. Add the breadcrumbs and fry gently for about 10 minutes, stirring frequently, until crisp and lightly golden.
2. In a bowl, mix together the sugar, sultanas, almonds and spices. Melt the remaining butter in a saucepan.
3. Brush one sheet of filo pastry all over with a little melted butter. Place another sheet of filo pastry on top and brush with melted butter.
4. Leaving a clear border of 4 cm (1½ inches) on all sides, sprinkle half the fried crumbs over the pastry. Arrange half the apple slices over the crumbs. Sprinkle with half the sugar and spice mixture.
5. Fold the four edges over the filling and brush with a little melted butter. Roll up the strudel, starting from a long edge.
6. Carefully form the roll into a slight horseshoe shape (without splitting) and place on a lightly greased baking sheet. Brush liberally with melted butter.
7. Cook in a preheated oven for 35-40 minutes until pastry is crisp and golden and filling is cooked through, brushing halfway through with melted butter. (Repeat points 3-7 for the second strudel.)
8. Cool slightly, then dust with sifted icing sugar. Serve with whipped cream.

BAKEWELL TART

Preparation time: 20 minutes, plus resting
Cooking time: 35 minutes
Oven: 190°C, 375°F, Gas Mark 5

½ quantity Pâte sablée (see below)
40 g (1½ oz) seedless raspberry jam
115 g (4 oz) caster sugar
2 eggs
115 g (4 oz) ground almonds
115 g (4 oz) unsalted butter, melted

1. Line a 20 cm (8 inch) flan ring with the pastry and prick the base.
2. Spread the jam evenly over the base.
3. Whisk the sugar and eggs in a mixing bowl until the mixture doubles in volume and leaves a trail when the whisk is lifted.
4. Using a metal spoon, fold in the almonds, then the melted butter. Work very delicately or the butter will fall during cooking and the tart will be stodgy.
5. Pour the mixture into the pastry case and bake in a preheated oven for 35 minutes, until the filling is well risen and golden brown.

PÂTE SABLÉE

Preparation time: 10 minutes, plus resting
Makes 675 g (1½ lb) pastry
Will line 2 × 20 cm (8 inch) flan rings

300 g (11 oz) plain flour
150 g (5½ oz) unsalted butter, chopped into small pieces
125 g (4½ oz) caster sugar
2 eggs

This pastry may be stored, foil-wrapped, in the refrigerator for five days.
1. Rub the flour and butter together in a mixing bowl until the mixture resembles fine breadcrumbs.
2. Lightly beat the sugar and egg and add to the butter and flour mixture. Work the paste into a smooth ball.
3. Rest for 30 minutes before use.

From the left: *Bakewell Tart, Apricot Tart*

PÂTE BRISÉE

Preparation time: 10 minutes, plus resting
Makes about 500 g (1¼ lb) pastry
Will line 2 × 20 cm (8 inch) flan rings

275 g (10 oz) plain flour
225 g (8 oz) unsalted butter, cut into 1 cm
(½ inch) cubes
2 teaspoons caster sugar
pinch of salt
1 egg, size 6, lightly beaten
approximately 1 tablespoon cold water

This pastry may be stored, foil-wrapped, in the refrigerator for 5 days.
1. Place the flour in a mixing bowl and make a well in the centre. Place the butter, sugar and salt in the well and mix lightly with the flour.
2. Add the egg and mix to a paste, handling as little as possible. Add a little water if necessary.
3. Transfer to a floured work surface and flatten the mixture using the heel of the hand. Fold in half, then in half again.
4. Work into a ball shape and rest for 1 hour.

LEMON MERINGUE PIE

Preparation time: 40 minutes, plus resting
Cooking time: 40 minutes
*Oven: 200°C, 400°F, Gas Mark 6; then 160°C,
325°F, Gas Mark 3*

3 lemons, scrubbed
200 ml (7 fl oz) boiling water
65 g (2½ oz) plain flour
75 g (3 oz) clear honey
75 g (3 oz) caster sugar
3 egg yolks
½ quantity Pâte brisée (see above)
Swiss meringue:
2 egg whites
120 g (4½ oz) caster sugar

*Opposite: Lemon
Meringue Pie*

1. Remove the zest of the lemons using a vegetable peeler. Infuse the peel in the boiling water for 4 minutes then strain.
2. Squeeze the lemons and combine the juice and the water in which the zest was infused.
3. Blend the flour with the liquid, then pour into a *stainless steel* or *enamel* pan and bring to the boil stirring continuously. Simmer until thickened.
4. Add the honey and sugar and bring to the boil.
5. Away from the heat, beat in the yolks and allow the mixture to cool.
6. Line a 20 cm (8 inch) flan ring with the pastry. Rest for 30 minutes. Bake blind for 20 minutes in a preheated oven. Remove the beans and greaseproof paper.
7. To make the Swiss meringue, whisk the egg whites until stiff. Gradually whisk in half the sugar until the mixture is thick and glossy, then carefully fold in the remaining sugar.
8. Pour the lemon cream into the pastry and spoon or pipe the meringue on top of the lemon cream.
9. Reduce the oven temperature and bake for a further 20 minutes. Cool slightly and remove the ring.

Variations:
1. Orange meringue pie: use 3 medium oranges or 3 tangerines in place of the lemons.
2. Lime meringue pie: use 2 limes and 1 lemon in place of the lemons.
3. Citrus meringue pie: use 1 lemon, 1 lime and 1 orange or tangerine in place of the lemons.

RHUBARB CRUMBLE FLAN

Preparation time: 30 minutes, plus chilling
Cooking time: 56 minutes
Oven: 190°C, 375°F, Gas Mark 5; then 180°C,
350°F, Gas Mark 4
Serves 6-8

½ quantity Pâte brisée (see page 100)
450 g (1 lb) rhubarb, trimmed and cut into
2.5 cm (1 inch) pieces
finely grated rind of 1 small orange
25 g (1 oz) ratafias, crumbled
50 g (2 oz) granulated sugar
75 g (3 oz) plain flour
25 g (1 oz) rolled oats
50 g (2 oz) hard margarine, diced
50 g (2 oz) demerara sugar
25 g (1 oz) bran flakes, coarsely crushed
40 g (1½ oz) chopped nuts

Illustrated on page 92

1. Roll out the prepared pâte brisée on a lightly floured work surface so it is large enough to line the base and sides of a 23 cm (9 inch) fluted flan dish. Trim the top edge neatly, then prick the pastry base all over with a fork. Line with greaseproof paper and fill with baking beans.
2. Place on a baking sheet. Cook in a preheated oven for 8 minutes. Remove the paper and beans and continue cooking for a further 8 minutes. Remove from oven.
3. Mix the rhubarb with the orange rind, ratafias and granulated sugar and spoon the mixture into the flan dish.
4. Put the flour and rolled oats into a bowl and rub in the fat fairly finely. Mix in the demerara sugar, bran flakes and nuts.
5. Spoon the topping over the fruit and flatten lightly. Cook in a preheated oven for 25 minutes, then reduce the oven temperature and continue cooking for a further 15 minutes until the topping is golden brown and the filling cooked through. Serve hot or cold with cream.

FRENCH APPLE TARTLETS

Preparation time: 40 minutes, plus chilling
Cooking time: 47 minutes
Oven: 190°C, 375°F, Gas Mark 5
Makes 4

2 cooking apples, peeled, cored and thinly
sliced
75 g (3 oz) caster sugar
15 g (½ oz) butter
½ quantity Pâte brisée (see page 100)
Topping:
2 small dessert apples, peeled, cored and
cut into 3 mm (⅛ inch) thick slices
1 tablespoon lemon juice
1 tablespoon granulated sugar
5 tablespoons apricot jam, sieved
1 tablespoon icing sugar

Illustrated on page 92

1. Put the cooking apples in a pan with the caster sugar and butter. Cover and cook gently for 10 minutes or until soft. Beat to a smooth purée. Cool.
2. Divide the pâte brisée into four. Knead each portion lightly, then roll out on a lightly floured work surface to rounds large enough to line the bases and sides of 4 × 11 cm (4½ inch) diameter, loose-based, fluted flan tins. Trim top edges and press pastry firmly into the flutes in the tins. Price the bases all over with a fork. Chill.
3. Spoon the cooled apple purée into the tins. Toss the dessert apple slices in lemon juice and arrange in overlapping circles on top of the purée. Sprinkle with sugar.
4. Place the flan tins on a baking sheet. Cook in a preheated oven for 35-40 minutes until the pastry is golden brown and the apple topping is cooked through.
5. Put the jam into a small pan and heat through gently until runny and smooth. Sprinkle the surfaces of the hot tartlets with sifted icing sugar and place under a preheated hot grill for 1-2 minutes, or until the apple slices are lightly golden.
6. Very carefully brush, or spoon, the hot jam over the hot tartlets. Leave to cool slightly before removing from tins.

MARSHMALLOW PIE

Preparation time: 45 minutes, plus chilling
Cooking time: 15 minutes
Serves 6-8

175 g (6 oz) digestive biscuits, crushed
75 g (3 oz) butter, melted
25 g (1 oz) demerara sugar
15 g (½ oz) gelatine
3 tablespoons water
225 g (8 oz) pink marshmallows
300 ml (½ pint) milk
75 g (3 oz) chopped walnuts
1 × 150 ml (5 fl oz) carton double cream
To decorate:
whipped cream
6 maraschino cherries

1. Place the biscuit crumbs in a bowl, and work in the melted butter and demerara sugar.
2. Use this mixture to line the base and sides of an 18 cm (7 inch) springform tin. Place in the refrigerator to set firm while making the filling.
3. Mix the gelatine with the water and allow it to melt over a low heat. Set aside to cool.
4. Roughly chop the marshmallows and place them with the milk in a saucepan. Heat the mixture gently, stirring, until the marshmallows have melted in the milk. Remove from the heat, stir in the gelatine and chopped nuts, and allow the mixture to cool until it just begins to set.
5. Whip the cream until it forms soft peaks and fold it into the marshmallow mixture.
6. Pour into the biscuit case and chill for at least 4 hours.
7. When ready to serve, remove the pie from the springform tin and place on a serving plate.
8. To decorate, place the cream in a piping bag and pipe 6 rosettes around the top of the cake, then place a maraschino cherry in the middle of each one.

Marshmallow Pie

TRADITIONAL PUDDINGS

Many traditional puddings and desserts are experiencing a new popularity, with nursery-style puddings being found on some of the smartest dinner party menus.

It is not really surprising that traditional puddings should be constant favourites, for who could ever resist a freshly-baked apple bursting with chopped nuts and dried fruit like figs; a slice of Jam Roly Poly nestling in a pool of hot creamy custard; pears moistly marinating in a wine-soaked syrup filled with crushed macaroons and ginger marmalade; or a wedge of Golden Treacle Sponge or Spotted Dick all the better for cream or custard?

Like all good classics and traditions, most of these recipes also seem to deny the constraints of seasonality – Chocolate Roulade, Crème Caramel and Queen of Puddings suit any time of year – and think-ahead cooks can score highly by popping a fruit-laden Summer Pudding or Bramble and Apple Pie in the freezer for the winter months.

Many of these popular and traditional puddings have been built upon the need to be thrifty or waste little. Summer Pudding, Bread and Butter Pudding, Spiced Bread Pudding and Queen of Puddings all make good use of fresh, day-old or stale bread in their make-up alongside everyday storecupboard items like eggs, butter, jam and sugar.

Continue the traditional theme when choosing the rest of your menu. Opt for classic and traditional starters like a good vegetable soup or the French onion soup, a shellfish cocktail or sliced smoked salmon. Suitable main courses include Lancashire hot pot, steak and kidney pudding, duck with cherries, boiled bacon with parsley sauce, game pie, fish pie or beef Wellington. Remember to contrast heartiness, texture, colour and flavours in your ultimate choice.

From the top: Apple and Gooseberry Charlotte (page 117), Summer Pudding (page 106), Jam Roly Poly with custard (page 106)

JAM ROLY POLY

Preparation time: 25-30 minutes
Cooking time: 50 minutes
Oven: 190°C, 375°F, Gas Mark 5
Serves 6-8

225 g (8 oz) self-raising flour
¼ teaspoon salt
100 g (4 oz) shredded suet
75 g (3 oz) fresh white breadcrumbs
150 ml (¼ pint) milk
10 tablespoons Morello cherry jam (or any jam of your choice)
10 g (¼ oz) butter, for greasing

Illustrated on page 104

1. Sift the flour and salt. Add the suet and 50 g (2 oz) of the breadcrumbs. Mix well. Add the milk and mix to a firm dough.
2. Roll out pastry on a lightly floured work surface to a rectangle measuring 25 × 30 cm (10 × 12 inches). Put the jam into a saucepan and heat gently until slightly runny. Spread 7 tablespoons of jam over the pastry, leaving a 2 cm (¾ inch) border all the way round. Sprinkle the remaining breadcrumbs over the jam.
3. Turn in the edges on the two long sides and one short side and brush all edges with water. Roll up the pastry, starting at the short side with a folded edge, neatly.
4. Place a large sheet of greased kitchen foil on a baking sheet. Lift the roll and place, join-side down on to the foil. Wrap the pudding in foil, with a centre pleat to allow for expansion. Twist the ends of the foil to seal well.
5. Cook just above centre in a preheated oven for 45 minutes until well risen and cooked.
6. Place the cooked roly poly on a warm serving plate and spoon over the remaining warmed jam. Serve hot with custard.

SUMMER PUDDING

Preparation time: 40 minutes, plus pressing
Cooking time: 5 minutes
Serves 6

10 slices of one-day-old white bread, crusts removed
3 tablespoons milk
750 g (1½ lb) mixed soft fruit (raspberries, redcurrants or white currants, strawberries and cherries if available)
100 g (4 oz) caster sugar

Illustrated on page 104

1. Lightly butter a 1 litre (1¾ pint) pudding basin.
2. Moisten the bread with the milk.
3. Hull, stone, or top and tail the fruit as necessary. Cook it very gently with the sugar for 4-5 minutes until the sugar melts and the juices run. Spoon off a few spoonfuls of the juice as it cools and reserve.
4. Line the sides and bottom of the basin with the bread slices. Reserve enough bread for the lid.
5. Pour in the fruit, which should come almost to the top. Cover closely with the remaining bread.
6. Put a small plate over the top (it should just fit inside the rim of the basin), and weight it with something heavy. Leave to press overnight in a cool place.
7. To serve, remove the weight and the plate. Place a serving plate over the top and reverse so the pudding comes out.
8. Pour the reserved juice slowly all over the pudding, especially where the juices might not have seeped through.
9. Keep cold until ready to use and serve with single cream.

ALMOND AND FIG BAKED APPLES

Preparation time: 15 minutes
Cooking time: 35 minutes
Oven: 180°C, 350°F, Gas Mark 4
Serves 6

6 Bramley cooking apples
50 g (2 oz) butter
400 g (14 oz) dried figs, chopped
6 tablespoons ground almonds
3 tablespoons sherry
cream or custard, to serve

This easily prepared dessert relies on the delicious flavour of Bramley cooking apples.

1. Wash and dry the apples and remove the cores. Make a circular cut around the waist of each apple. Place in a roasting tin.
2. Melt half the butter in a small saucepan and add the figs, half the almonds and the sherry. Stir over a high heat for 5 minutes.
3. Fill the apples with this mixture and top each one with a little of the remaining butter and almonds.
4. Cook in a preheated oven for 25-30 minutes, depending on the size of the apple.
5. Serve with cream or custard.

Variation: There are endless different stuffings for baked apples. Keep your fillings tasty but reasonably dry, then use honey, golden syrup, treacle or maple syrup to pour over the apples during the cooking. Baste the apples with the juices during the cooking period.

Almond and Fig Baked Apples

BREAD AND BUTTER PUDDING

Preparation time: 10 minutes, plus soaking
Cooking time: about 55-60 minutes
Oven: 180°C, 350°F, Gas Mark 4; then 190°C,
375°F, Gas Mark 5

40 g (1½ oz) butter
4 slices white bread, crusts removed
4 tablespoons apricot jam
25 g (1 oz) cut mixed peel
25 g (1 oz) sultanas
450 ml (¾ pint) milk
2 tablespoons sugar
2 eggs, beaten

1. Use 15 g (½ oz) of the butter to grease a 1.2 litre (2 pint) ovenproof serving dish.
2. Butter the bread and spread with apricot jam. Cut into small triangles. Layer the bread in the dish, sprinkling mixed peel and sultanas between the layers.
3. Heat the milk and sugar to just below boiling point. Whisk in the eggs, then strain over the bread and butter. Leave to soak for 30 minutes.
4. Place the dish in a water bath (a roasting tin with water to come at least halfway up the sides of the dish). Bake in a preheated oven for 45 minutes, then increase the heat and cook for a further 10-15 minutes until crisp and golden on top and just set. Serve at once.

SPICED BREAD PUDDING

Preparation time: 5 minutes, plus soaking
Cooking time: 45 minutes
Oven: 180°C, 350°F, Gas Mark 4
Serves 6-8

225 g (8 oz) stale granary bread, cubed
450 ml (¾ pint) milk
50 g (2 oz) butter
50 g (2 oz) demerara sugar
50 g (2 oz) sultanas
50 g (2 oz) currants
1 teaspoon ground cinnamon
1 teaspoon ground ginger
½ teaspoon ground nutmeg
2 eggs, beaten

1. Place the bread in a mixing bowl. Bring the milk, butter and sugar to the boil and pour over the bread. Mix well and leave to soak for 15 minutes, stirring the mixture occasionally.
2. Add the remaining ingredients and beat well until evenly mixed.
3. Spoon into a buttered 28 × 18 cm (11 × 7 inch) ovenproof baking dish and bake in a preheated oven for 45 minutes until golden and firm to the touch. Sprinkle with demerara sugar and serve cut in squares.

BAKED PEARS IN WHITE WINE

Preparation time: 15 minutes
Cooking time: 20-30 minutes
Oven: 180°C, 350°F, Gas Mark 4
Serves 6

50 g (2 oz) butter
6 large ripe pears (preferably Conference)
peeled, halved and cored
6 tablespoons ginger marmalade
6 tablespoons roughly crushed macaroons
300 ml (½ pint) sweet white wine

1. Use a quarter of the butter to grease a large, shallow ovenproof dish, just large enough to hold the pears in a single layer.
2. Place the pear halves in the dish, cut side up, and fill the hollows with ginger marmalade and the crushed macaroons.
3. Pour the wine around the pears, dot them with the remaining butter and bake in a preheated oven for 20-30 minutes until just tender when tested with a skewer.

Clockwise from top left: Spiced Bread Pudding, Bread and Butter Pudding, Baked Pears in White Wine

GOLDEN TREACLE SPONGE

Preparation time: 20 minutes
Cooking time: 1½ hours
Serves 4-6

100 g (4 oz) butter
100 g (4 oz) caster sugar
grated rind of 1 orange
2 eggs, beaten
150 g (5 oz) self-raising flour
4 tablespoons golden syrup

1. Grease a 900 ml (1½ pint) pudding basin.
2. Cream the butter, sugar and orange rind together until they are light and fluffy.
3. Add the eggs gradually and beat well between each addition.
4. Sift the flour and fold it into the mixture.
5. Spoon the syrup into the bottom of the pudding basin and pour the sponge mixture on top.
6. Cover the basin with a pleated piece of greased, greaseproof paper and aluminium foil large enough to allow for expansion and tie with string.
7. Place the basin in a heavy saucepan, two-thirds full of hot water, cover and steam steadily over a low heat for approximately 1½ hours. Top up with hot water if necessary during the cooking time.
8. To serve, remove the string, paper and foil and turn the sponge out on to a warmed dish. Serve with custard.

STEAMED CHOCOLATE SPONGE

Preparation time: 30 minutes
Cooking time: 1½ hours
Serves 4-6

100 g (4 oz) butter
100 g (4 oz) caster sugar
2 eggs, beaten
150 g (5 oz) self-raising flour
20 g (¾ oz) cocoa powder mixed with 2 tablespoons milk

1. Grease a 900 ml (1½ pint) pudding basin.
2. Cream the butter and sugar together in a mixing bowl until they are light and fluffy.
3. Add the eggs gradually and beat well between each addition.
4. Sift the flour and fold it in using a figure of eight motion until thoroughly blended. Add the cocoa mixed with milk.
5. Spoon the sponge mixture into the pudding basin.
6. Cover the basin with a pleated piece of greased greaseproof paper and aluminium foil large enough to allow for expansion, and tie with string.
7. Place the basin in a heavy saucepan, two-thirds full of hot water, cover and steam steadily over a low heat for approximately 1½ hours. Top up with hot water if necessary during the cooking time.
8. To serve, remove the string, paper and foil and turn the pudding out on to a warmed dish. Serve the pudding with a chocolate sauce, if liked.

QUEEN OF PUDDINGS

Preparation time: 30 minutes, plus soaking
Cooking time: 50-60 minutes
Oven: 180°C, 350°F, Gas Mark 4
Serves 6

300 ml (½ pint) milk
200 g (7 oz) caster sugar
3 eggs, separated
a few drops of vanilla essence
75 g (3 oz) fresh white breadcrumbs
3 tablespoons raspberry jam
juice of ½ lemon

1. Put the milk, 25 g (1 oz) of the sugar, egg yolks and vanilla essence in a mixing bowl and whisk together.
2. Pour the mixture over the breadcrumbs and leave for 15 minutes.
3. Transfer to a 900 ml (1½ pint) greased ovenproof dish and bake in a preheated oven for 30 minutes.
4. Remove from the oven and leave to cool slightly.
5. Mix the jam and lemon juice together and spread evenly over the surface of the pudding.
6. Beat the egg whites until they are stiff. Add the remaining sugar a tablespoon at a time, whisking well between each addition until the mixture is thick and glossy.
7. Pipe or spoon the meringue on top of the pudding and return to the oven for about 20 minutes until the meringue is crisp and lightly coloured. Serve the Queen of Puddings hot.

From the left: *Golden Treacle Sponge, Steamed Chocolate Pudding, Queen of Puddings*

BRAMBLE AND APPLE PIE

Preparation time: 20 minutes, plus chilling
Cooking time: 55-60 minutes
Oven: 220°C, 425°F, Gas Mark 7; then 190°C,
375°F, Gas Mark 5
Serves 6

Pastry:
275 g (10 oz) plain flour
¼ teaspoon salt
75 g (3 oz) hard margarine, cut into small
pieces
75 g (3 oz) white fat, cut into small pieces
3 tablespoons cold water
Filling:
1 kg (2 lb) cooking apples, peeled, cored
and thinly sliced
225 g (8 oz) blackberries
75 g (3 oz) sugar
1 tablespoon cornflour
1 tablespoon cold water
1 tablespoon golden syrup
10 g (¼ oz) butter, cut into small pieces
To finish:
beaten egg, to glaze
1-2 teaspoons sugar

1. Make the pastry: put the flour and salt into a mixing bowl, add the fats and rub in until the mixture resembles fine breadcrumbs. Stir in the water all at once, and mix quickly with a round-bladed knife to form a fairly firm dough.
2. Knead the dough gently on a lightly floured work surface until smooth and free from cracks. Chill.
3. Put the apple slices and blackberries in a bowl. Mix the sugar and cornflour together and stir into the fruit.
4. Put the fruit into a 1.2 litre (2 pint) pie dish. Add the water and golden syrup and dot with pieces of butter.
5. Cut off a quarter of the dough and reserve for decoration. Roll out the remaining dough on a lightly-floured surface to about 5 mm (¼ inch) thickness and 2.5 cm (1 inch) larger all round than the size of the pie dish.
6. Cut off a strip of pastry wide enough to cover the pie dish rim. Dampen the rim and press the pastry strip in position. Dampen the pastry strip and cover with the pastry lid, sealing the edges together well.
7. Trim the edges, then knock up with the back of a knife and flute the edges at 1 cm (½ inch) intervals. Make a small hole in the centre of the pie.
8. Roll out the reserved pastry and make into leaves. [F]
9. Brush the surface of the pie with beaten egg. Arrange the pastry leaves in position and brush with beaten egg. Sprinkle the pie with sugar.
10. Put the pie dish on a baking sheet and cook in a preheated oven for 25 minutes until the pastry is lightly golden, then reduce the oven temperature and continue cooking for a further 25-30 minutes until the fruit is tender and cooked through. Cover with foil during cooking if necessary to prevent overbrowning.
11. Serve hot or cold with custard or cream.

[F] The unglazed pie can be frozen for up to 3 months. Thaw for several hours at room temperature or overnight in the refrigerator.

SPOTTED DICK

Preparation time: 10 minutes
Cooking time: 3 hours
Serves 6

175 g (6 oz) self-raising flour
pinch of salt
50 g (2 oz) fresh white breadcrumbs
100 g (4 oz) shredded suet
50 g (2 oz) caster sugar
175 g (6 oz) raisins or sultanas (or a mixture of both)
¼ teaspoon ground mixed spice
8 tablespoons milk
a little caster sugar, to finish

1. Put a large saucepan half-filled with water on to boil.
2. Put the flour, salt, breadcrumbs, suet, sugar, raisins or sultanas and mixed spice into a bowl and mix well together.
3. Add the milk and mix to form a fairly soft dough. On a lightly-floured work surface, form the dough into a roll about 16 cm (6½ inches) long and 9 cm (3½ inches) wide.
4. Wrap the roll loosely in greased greaseproof paper and foil, with a pleat in the centre to allow for expansion. Seal really well at the top and at either end to enclose completely.
5. Place in the top half of a steamer which will fit over the pan of boiling water or directly in the pan for 3 hours until well risen and cooked through. Top up the steamer or pan with boiling water as necessary during cooking.
6. Unwrap carefully and place the roll on a hot serving dish. Sprinkle with caster sugar, cut into slices and serve at once with custard.

Bramble and Apple Pie, Spotted Dick

CHOCOLATE ROULADE

Preparation time: 20-25 minutes
Cooking time: 10-12 minutes
Oven: 200°C, 400°F, Gas Mark 6
Serves 4-6

3 large eggs, separated
1 tablespoon warm water
75 g (3 oz) caster sugar
75 g (3 oz) plain flour
25 g (1 oz) cocoa powder
few drops of vanilla essence
caster sugar to sprinkle
Filling:
150 ml (¼ pint) whipping cream
4 × 60 g (2½ oz) cartons strawberry or
apricot fromage frais
2 teaspoons clear honey

1. Line a 35 × 25 cm (14 × 10 inch) Swiss roll tin with greaseproof paper. Grease liberally and dust with a little flour.
2. Whisk the egg whites with the water until very stiff. Gradually add the sugar, a spoonful at a time, whisking until thick and glossy. Whisk in the egg yolks, blending thoroughly.
3. Sift the flour with the cocoa and sift again over the egg mixture. Fold in carefully but thoroughly with a metal spoon. Fold in the vanilla essence. Turn the mixture into the prepared tin and level the surface. Bake in a preheated oven for 10-12 minutes.
4. When cooked, turn out quickly on to a sheet of greaseproof paper generously sprinkled with caster sugar. Trim away the hard edges of the roll with a sharp knife and roll up, from one of the shorter ends, enclosing the greaseproof paper. Leave until cold.
5. Meanwhile, to make the filling, whip the cream until it stands in soft peaks. Fold in the fromage frais and honey, blending well.
6. Unroll the roulade and carefully remove the greaseproof paper. Spread generously with the cream mixture and re-roll. Dust with a little extra sugar before serving.

CRÈME CARAMEL

Preparation time: 10-12 minutes, plus chilling
Cooking time: 1 hour-1 hour 15 minutes
Oven: 160°C, 325°F, Gas Mark 3

50 g (2 oz) granulated sugar
2 tablespoons cold water
2 tablespoons boiling water
300 ml (½ pint) creamy milk
4 eggs, beaten
25 g (1 oz) caster sugar
few drops of vanilla essence
orange zest, to garnish (optional)

1. Place the sugar in a pan with the cold water. Slowly bring to the boil, ensuring that the sugar has dissolved. Boil quickly over a high heat until the mixture turns a rich golden brown. Quickly, and taking care to avoid spitting, add the boiling water. Pour into a greased 600 ml (1 pint) ovenproof dish and swirl to coat the base.
2. Place the milk in a pan and heat until hot but not boiling. Pour over the eggs and beat well to combine. Add the sugar and vanilla to taste, blending well. Strain through a nylon sieve over the caramel mixture.
3. Put the dish in a bain-marie or roasting pan with sufficient hot water to come half-way up the sides of the dish. Bake in a preheated oven for about 50 minutes or until set. Allow to cool then chill.
4. To serve, invert on to a plate and shake gently to release. Serve lightly chilled and garnished with orange zest, if liked.

From the left: *Chocolate Roulade, Crème Caramel*

Christmas Pudding

CHRISTMAS PUDDING

Preparation time: 20 minutes
Cooking time: 10-11 hours, including
re-heating
Makes 2 × 1 kg/2 lb puddings

450 g (1 lb) fresh white breadcrumbs
225 g (8 oz) shredded suet
225 g (8 oz) dark molasses sugar
1 teaspoon ground ginger
1 teaspoon ground cinnamon
½ teaspoon salt
225 g (8 oz) seedless raisins
225 g (8 oz) sultanas
225 g (8 oz) currants
50 g (2 oz) mixed candied peel, chopped
50 g (2 oz) glacé cherries, chopped
50 g (2 oz) blanched almonds, chopped
1 cooking apple, peeled, cored and grated
2 tablespoons golden syrup
2 tablespoons brandy
3 eggs, lightly beaten
150 ml (¼ pint) milk, to mix

This light-textured pudding is a useful recipe because it should be made only a few days before required. Remember, however, that the mixture improves if left to stand overnight.

1. Put all the dry ingredients in a bowl and stir well to mix. Add the apple, golden syrup, brandy and eggs, then enough milk to give a soft dropping consistency. Cover and leave to stand overnight.

2. The next day, spoon the mixture into buttered pudding basins, pressing it down well. Leave room for the puddings to rise during steaming. Cover with circles of buttered greaseproof paper, then cover with pudding cloth or foil and tie securely.

3. Place the puddings in the top of a steamer or double boiler, or in a pan half-filled with gently bubbling water. Cover with a lid, then steam for 8 hours, topping up the water level in the pan as necessary.

4. Remove the puddings from the pan and discard the cloth or foil and the greaseproof paper. Leave until cold, then cover with fresh greaseproof and cloth or foil. Store in a cool dry place for up to 1 week, then steam again for 2 to 3 hours before serving.

APPLE AND GOOSEBERRY CHARLOTTE

Preparation time: 20 minutes
Cooking time: 1 hour 20 minutes
Oven: 190°C, 375°F, Gas Mark 5; then 180°C,
350°F, Gas Mark 4
Serves 4-6

750 g (1½ lb) cooking apples, peeled, cored
and thinly sliced
225 g (8 oz) gooseberries, topped and tailed
175 g (6 oz) butter
175 g (6 oz) granulated sugar
8 large thin slices white bread, crusts
removed
1 tablespoon demerara sugar

Illustrated on page 104

1. Put the sliced apples, gooseberries and 50 g (2 oz) butter in a saucepan. Add the sugar and simmer gently for 25-30 minutes until almost no syrupy liquid remains, stirring frequently.
2. Melt 50 g (2 oz) of the remaining butter in a large frying pan. Cut the slices of bread in half to give 16 strips. Add half the bread strips to the melted butter and turn until coated all over. Fry over medium heat for 2-3 minutes, turning frequently until lightly golden on both sides. Remove the bread strips from pan and keep on one side. Repeat this process again using the remaining butter and bread strips.
3. Line the base and sides of a straight-sided ovenproof dish with about 10 of the bread strips. Spoon the apple mixture into the centre and level the surface. Cover with the remaining 6 strips of bread and press down firmly. Sprinkle the surface with demerara sugar. [A]
4. Cook in a preheated oven for 15 minutes, then reduce oven temperature and cover the surface of the charlotte with foil. Continue cooking for a further 25-30 minutes until golden brown all over. Run a knife around the edge of the charlotte and turn out on to a serving plate. (The charlotte may be served from the dish, if preferred.) Serve hot with cream.

[A] Can be prepared several hours in advance and stored in the refrigerator.

Variation: Frozen gooseberries may be used when fresh are unavailable, thawing them on absorbent paper before cooking with sliced apples.

FRUITY DESSERTS

**From the humble to the unusual and exotic, there is a
wealth of rich and zesty or mild and mellow fruity
desserts to choose from.**

Mix and match a whole host of berry fruits for a Summer Fruit
Salad; skewered pieces of melon, grapes and strawberries with
a rich chocolatey sauce for an unforgettable fondue; rhubarb
with orange juice, frothy egg whites and creamy yogurt for a
splendid fruit whip; and ripe peaches with colourful glacé
cherries topped with light-as-air brown sugar meringue
crisply-baked.

There is a fruit in season every month of the year. During the
spring and winter months when home-grown fruit can be thin
on the ground opt for Apple Salad Cups, Fruit-Stuffed
Pancakes, or Caramel Oranges, leaving the summer and
autumn abundant crop of stoned, berry and soft fruits for
making Fruited Crème Brûlée and Figs with Lemon Cream.

Look no further than recipes like Pears with Grenadine and
Baked Stuffed Peaches to use up any surplus fruits that have
not been eaten fresh. Many of these fruits can be quickly sliced
and sugared, gently cooked in syrup or chopped and puréed
for freezer storage, then used later in an infinite number of
fruity pudding and dessert recipes.

Most fruity desserts can be mixed and matched with almost
any starter or main course selection, provided that fruit isn't
too prominent a feature of it. If you are planning a rich fruity
dessert then light starters to choose from could include a
Chinese-style soup, a mousse-like Liver and Mushroom Pâté,
ceviche or piquant vegetable salad like courgette. If the dessert
is on the lean side, indulge in more substantial creamy soups,
coarse-textured rich game or meat terrines or rich pancake
starters. Ideal main courses that do not weigh heavily with
fruit include Spaghetti Bolognese, crown roast of lamb,
tandoori chicken and Beef Stroganoff.

*From the top: Chocolate
Fondue with Fruit
Kebabs (page 123),
Caramel Oranges (page
130), Fruited Crème
Brûlée (page 120)*

FRUITED CRÈME BRULÉE

Preparation time: 20 minutes, plus chilling
Cooking time: 1 hour
Oven: 150°C, 300°F, Gas Mark 2
Serves 4-5

4 egg yolks
25 g (1 oz) caster sugar
¼ teaspoon vanilla essence
300 ml (½ pint) double cream
100 g (4 oz) mixture blackcurrants and
raspberries, topped and tailed, and hulled
To finish:
50 g (2 oz) demerara sugar
To decorate:
raspberries
sprig of mint

Illustrated on page 118

1. Put the egg yolks, caster sugar and vanilla essence in a bowl and whisk well until the mixture is light and smooth.
2. Heat the cream very gently in a saucepan until hot (do not allow to boil). Pour the hot cream on to the egg yolk mixture, whisking well all the time.
3. Arrange the fruits in a 750-900 ml (1¼-1½ pint) shallow flameproof dish. Strain the cream mixture on top. Stand the dish in a roasting tin filled with sufficient cold water to come halfway up the sides of the dish.
4. Cook in a preheated oven for 50 minutes until the mixture is set, covering with foil during cooking to prevent the surface from browning. Cool, then chill overnight.
5. About 4 hours before serving, sprinkle the surface of the custard evenly with the demerara sugar. Place under a preheated hot grill for 5-7 minutes or until the sugar melts and caramelises to form a glaze, turning the dish frequently to brown the surface evenly. Allow to cool, then chill for at least 3 hours before serving decorated with raspberries and a sprig of mint.

SUMMER FRUIT SALAD

Preparation time: 15 minutes
Cooking time: 5 minutes
Serves 8

175 g (6 oz) caster sugar
300 ml (½ pint) water
450 g (1 lb) blackcurrants
225 g (8 oz) raspberries
450 g (1 lb) cherries, stoned
3 tablespoons Cassis
225 g (8 oz) strawberries

1. Dissolve the sugar in the water, add the blackcurrants. Simmer gently for about 5 minutes until the fruit is soft.
2. Pour into a large bowl, add the raspberries, cherries and Cassis. Chill well. Just before serving lightly stir in the strawberries.

Summer Fruit Salad

120

KIWI FRUIT, MANGO AND DATES SALAD

Preparation time: 20 minutes
Serves 6

6 kiwi fruit
3 mangoes
1 box fresh dates, stoned

1. Peel the kiwi fruit and slice across fairly thickly.
2. Peel the mangoes as thinly as possible. Slice them in large thin slices, rather than in 'canned peach' slices.
3. Either mix with the dates in a large glass bowl or arrange a selection of the 3 on 6 dessert plates, putting the dates shiny-side up.

CHOCOLATE FONDUE WITH FRUIT KEBABS

Preparation time: 15 minutes
Cooking time: 12-15 minutes
Serves 4-6

1 × 410 g (14½ oz) can evaporated milk
25 g (1 oz) caster sugar
175 g (6 oz) plain chocolate, grated or very finely chopped
2 tablespoons orange juice
To serve:
bite-sized pieces of melon; seedless grapes; whole strawberries, pink marshmallows

Illustrated on page 118

1. Put the evaporated milk, sugar and chocolate into a metal fondue pot. Heat slowly over a lighted spirit burner, stirring until the chocolate melts.
2. Bring to the boil, then reduce the heat and simmer for 5 minutes, stirring frequently. Add the orange juice, stir well and continue simmering until the mixture thickens sufficiently to coat the back of a spoon. Stir frequently during this time.
3. Meanwhile, spear the prepared fruits on to 12 short bamboo skewers and thread a marshmallow on to one end of each skewer.
4. As soon as the chocolate mixture reaches the 'coating stage', serve at once. Dip the prepared skewers into the chocolate mixture and swirl to coat.

Variation: Omit the orange juice and add instead 2 tablespoons brandy or Cointreau.
Note: This fondue can also be made very successfully in a saucepan, if you do not have a fondue pot. Fondue forks instead of bamboo skewers may be used for spearing and 'dipping' individual items, if preferred.

Opposite: Kiwi Fruit, Mango and Dates Salad

PEARS IN GRENADINE

Preparation time: 30 minutes
Cooking time: 40 minutes, plus overnight
soaking
Serves 6

6 firm pears, peeled and left whole
450 ml (¾ pint) grenadine syrup
750 ml (1¼ pints) water
1 teaspoon ground cloves
1 teaspoon ground cinnamon
1 teaspoon ground nutmeg
juice of 1 lemon
225 g (8 oz) sugar
To serve:
vanilla ice cream or double or whipping
cream, lightly whipped

Grenadine is a red syrup made of pomegranates. It is non-alcoholic, and is stocked by good quality drink shops and grocers.

1. Place the peeled pears in a saucepan large enough for them all to rest on the base. Mix together the grenadine and water and pour over the pears.
2. Add the cloves, cinnamon, nutmeg and lemon juice, then bring slowly to the boil. Simmer for 2-3 minutes, then remove from the heat and leave overnight to allow the pears to soak up the marinade.
3. Remove the pears and arrange on a serving dish.
4. Strain the marinade into a clean saucepan, and cook rapidly until the liquid has reduced by half.
5. Add the sugar and stir over a gentle heat until dissolved, then boil again until a syrup is obtained. (A sugar thermometer should register 107°C, 225°F or the syrup should form a fine, thin thread if allowed to fall from a spoon on to a dish.)
6. Cool the syrup and pour over the pears. Allow to cool completely before serving with ice cream or cream.

YOGURT FRUIT WHIP

Preparation time: 10-15 minutes, plus setting
Cooking time: 2 minutes
Serves 6

15 g (½ oz) powdered gelatine
150 ml (¼ pint) fresh or unsweetened
orange juice, at room temperature
2 teaspoons caster sugar
300 ml (½ pint) low-fat rhubarb yogurt, at
room temperature
2 egg whites
To decorate:
strips of thinly pared orange rind
(optional)

Illustrated on page 127

A delicately flavoured, light dessert to enjoy after a rich main course. Remove from the refrigerator 30 minutes before serving, to appreciate the subtle flavour.
1. Sprinkle the gelatine over 2 tablespoons of the orange juice in a small heatproof bowl and leave to soften for 10 minutes until spongy. Stand the bowl in a saucepan of simmering water and leave until the gelatine dissolves. Stir in the sugar, then remove from the heat and leave to cool for about 6 minutes; do not allow to set.
2. Place the remaining orange juice, yogurt and cooled liquid gelatine in a blender goblet and blend for 30 seconds until thoroughly combined and smooth. Pour the mixture into a bowl and leave for about 20-30 minutes until just beginning to set around the edges.
3. Whisk the egg whites until stiff peaks form. Using a large metal spoon, lightly fold them into the yogurt mixture until well incorporated. Spoon the mixture into a serving bowl and leave for 2-3 hours to set in the refrigerator. Decorate with strips of orange rind, if liked, and serve with dainty sweet biscuits.

APPLE SALAD CUPS

Preparation time: 20 minutes

4 large red dessert apples
1 tablespoon lemon juice
1 small banana, peeled, quartered and
sliced
50 g (2 oz) sultanas
25 g (1 oz) flaked almonds, chopped
3 tablespoon diced melon (optional)
150 ml (¼ pint) black cherry yogurt

Illustrated on page 126

Encourage children to eat more fruit by
serving these pretty little salads.
1. Cut a thin slice off each apple at the
flower end. Using a serrated grapefruit
knife or small sharp knife, carefully scoop
out the apple flesh, cutting to within 5 mm
(¼ inch) of the edge of each apple. Discard
the cores. Cut the apple flesh into small
dice and place in a bowl.
2. Brush the insides of the apple shells
with lemon juice and sprinkle the
remainder over the diced apple. Toss well
to prevent the apple from discolouring. **A**
3. Add the banana, sultanas, almonds and
melon, if using, to the apple. Stir in the
yogurt and lightly mix together. Spoon the
fruit mixture into the apple shells and
serve immediately.

A The Apple Salad Cups can be prepared
up to 1 hour in advance, covered with cling
film and kept in a cool place.

Pears in Grenadine

From the left: Apple Salad Cups (page 125), Peachy Almond Meringues, Buttered Bananas with Pineapple Cream Sauce, Yogurt Fruit Whip (page 124)

PEACHY ALMOND MERINGUES

Preparation time: 10 minutes
Cooking time: 15 minutes
Oven: 190°C, 375°F, Gas Mark 5
Serves 4-6

4 ripe peaches, peeled and halved
10 g (¼ oz) butter
8 maraschino or glacé cherries
3 egg whites
75 g (3 oz) ground almonds
75 g (3 oz) soft light brown sugar

1. Arrange the peach halves cut side up in a buttered shallow ovenproof dish. Place a cherry in the middle of each peach half.
2. Whisk the egg whites until stiff peaks form. Using a large metal spoon, lightly and carefully fold the ground almonds and sugar into the whisked egg whites.
3. Spoon the almond meringue over the peach halves. Bake in a preheated oven for 15 minutes or until the meringue is set and golden brown. Serve hot with ice cream.

Variation: Canned peach halves can be used instead of fresh peaches; pat dry on absorbent paper before placing in the dish. Heat the peach syrup from the can in a small saucepan and hand separately.

BUTTERED BANANAS WITH PINEAPPLE CREAM SAUCE

Preparation time: 5 minutes
Cooking time: 7 minutes

4 medium bananas, peeled and halved
lengthways
2 tablespoons soft light brown sugar
40 g (1½ oz) butter
150 ml (¼ pint) unsweetened pineapple
juice
150 ml (¼ pint) single cream
1 tablespoon chopped mixed nuts, to
decorate

A deliciously rich dessert made in a matter of moments from a few simple ingredients.
1. Roll the bananas in the sugar. Melt the butter in a large frying pan until foaming, then add the bananas and fry over a moderate heat for about 3-4 minutes, turning occasionally, until the sugar begins to caramelize. Carefully transfer the bananas to a warmed serving dish and keep warm.
2. Pour the pineapple juice into the pan, bring to the boil and boil for 2 minutes, stirring constantly. Stir in the cream and boil for a further 5 minutes or until the sauce is thickened and smooth. Spoon the hot sauce over the bananas and sprinkle with nuts. Serve hot.

BAKED STUFFED PEACHES

Preparation time: 15 minutes
Cooking time: 30-35 minutes
Oven: 190°C, 375°F, Gas Mark 5

4 firm ripe peaches, peeled, cut in half and stoned
4 stale macaroons, crushed
1 tablespoon ground almonds
2 tablespoons mixed crystallized fruits, finely chopped
1 egg yolk
150 ml (¼ pint) double or whipping cream
1 tablespoon Kirsch or rum (optional)
40 g (1½ oz) icing sugar
40 g (1½ oz) unsalted butter, melted
2 tablespoons water
To finish:
2-3 tablespoons Kirsch or rum (optional)

1. With a teaspoon, scoop out a little flesh from the centre of each peach half. Chop this up and mix with the macaroons, ground almonds, crystallized fruits, egg yolk, 1 tablespoon cream and 1 tablespoon Kirsch or rum if using. Stuff the peach halves with this mixture and place in a buttered fireproof dish.
2. Sprinkle the icing sugar over the top of each and brush the outsides with the melted butter. Sprinkle the rest of the butter over the top of the peaches.
3. Add 2 tablespoons water to the dish and cook in a preheated oven for 25-30 minutes, until the peaches are cooked.
4. Beat the remaining cream until it stands in soft peaks and place in a serving dish.
5. When the peaches are cooked arrange them in a fireproof serving dish, warm the Kirsch or rum, if using, pour over the peaches and ignite. Serve immediately, with the whipped cream.

FRUIT-STUFFED PANCAKES

Preparation time: 30 minutes
Cooking time: 30-40 minutes

Pancakes:
150 g (5 oz) plain flour
¼ teaspoon salt
2 eggs
300 ml (½ pint) milk
1 tablespoon oil
oil, for cooking
Fruit filling:
2 oranges
300 ml (½ pint) Crème patissière
(see page 98)
1 kiwi fruit, peeled and sliced
1-2 tablespoons sieved icing sugar

1. To make the pancakes, sift the flour and salt into a bowl and make a well in the centre. Break in the eggs and add half the milk. Beat in the flour from the sides of the bowl until a smooth thick batter is obtained. Gradually add the remaining milk. **A**
2. Heat a little oil in a frying pan, then pour it off, leaving a thin film on the base of the pan. Pour in batter just to cover the base of the pan, tipping the pan to ensure an even, thin coating. When bubbles appear on the surface and the underside has browned, turn the pancake over with a spatula and cook on the other side for 1-2 minutes.
3. Make 4 large or 8 small pancakes in all and keep hot. **A** **F**
4. Grate the rind from one orange, and with a sharp serrated knife cut off the pith and carefully remove the segments of orange. Cut each segment into 2-3 pieces. Thinly slice the other orange.
5. Make the Crème patissière, adding the grated rind to the milk. When it is thick, add the chopped orange pieces.
6. Place some of the cream down the centre of each pancake and roll up. Arrange on a hot serving dish.
7. Just before serving, sprinkle a little icing sugar over the top. Garnish with sliced oranges and kiwi fruit.

A Either the batter or the pancakes can be made earlier in the day.
F Pancakes can be frozen, sandwiched between sheets of greaseproof paper. If many are needed, defrost at room temperature. A few can be defrosted and reheated over hot water. Once they have been taken out of the freezer and separated, they defrost very quickly.

Variations: Heat 2-3 tablespoons orange jelly marmalade and pour over the pancakes instead of the icing sugar. Flambé the pancakes, which should be placed in a fireproof dish, with Cointreau, Grand Marnier or other orange-flavoured liqueur.

From the left: Baked Stuffed Peaches, Fruit-Stuffed Pancakes

FIGS WITH LEMON CREAM

Preparation time: 20 minutes, plus chilling

8 fresh, ripe figs
1 teaspoon caster sugar
juice of 1 lemon
175 ml (6 fl oz) double cream
8 sprigs of mint, to decorate

1. Peel the figs if preferred, and cut a cross on the top of each one.
2. Press gently to open the cross (as one would do a baked potato).
3. Arrange the figs on a serving dish and chill for 1 hour.
4. Dissolve the sugar in the lemon juice and slowly stir in the cream. Adding the cream slowly to the sweetened lemon juice will thicken the cream.
5. Spoon the cream into the figs, and decorate with sprigs of mint.

CARAMEL ORANGES

Preparation time: 20 minutes, plus chilling
Cooking time: 8-9 minutes
Serves 6

175 g (6 oz) granulated sugar
150 ml (¼ pint) cold water
150 ml (¼ pint) warm water
6 oranges (preferably seedless)

Illustrated on page 118

1. Put the sugar and cold water in a small saucepan and heat gently, stirring to dissolve the sugar. Bring to the boil and boil for 7-8 minutes or until the syrup turns a rich caramel colour.
2. Remove from the heat. Hold the pan handle with a cloth (as the mixture will splutter when warm water is added). Add warm water to the pan and wait a few moments for the spluttering to stop. Return the pan to the heat and heat through for 1-2 minutes, stirring all the time. Remove from the heat and leave to cool.
3. Using a potato peeler, peel off several very thin strips of orange rind and cut them into very fine matchstick strips. Cook the strips in boiling water for 2 minutes. Drain, then cover with cold water and reserve for decoration.
4. Peel the oranges, using a sharp knife, removing all the bitter white pith. Cut the oranges into 5 mm (¼ inch) thick slices and then secure the slices together, using cocktail sticks, to form whole oranges again.
5. Arrange the oranges in a serving dish. Pour over the cooled caramel syrup and chill for several hours, before serving. Turn the oranges in the syrup several times during chilling.
6. Drain the orange peel strips and pat dry on absorbent kitchen paper. Sprinkle the orange strips over the oranges. Serve chilled with pouring cream.

Opposite: Figs with Lemon Cream

CHEESECAKES & GÂTEAUX

Cheesecakes, whether rich and creamy or light and delicate, are comparative newcomers to the desserts scene, while gâteaux are old favourites.

———————— ⚜ ————————

Most cheesecakes are made with cottage cheese, curd cheese or cream cheese, but with the ever-increasing variety of soft, calorie and fat-reduced cheeses now available they can be made lighter, healthier and more suitable for the slimming or dieting fraternity. Even the cream content can be altered by using fat-reduced creams, fromage frais, yogurt and fruit cheeses for part of the quantity.

Among the gâteaux here are a good sprinkling of the classics: Gâteau St Honoré with its crisp base of short pastry and choux-topped ring of tiny buns filled with cream and glazing with a rich caramel; Nectarine Vacherin, a crisp gâteau of discs of hazelnut meringue sandwiched with cream and nectarines; and Cherry Gâteau Cardinale, a sponge-layered treat of cherries with cream and almonds. You'll also find some new ideas. Try Black Cherry Gâteau which makes a delicious change from the usual Black Forest variety; and Strawberry and Orange Gâteau which has been developed with summer very much in mind, although frozen strawberries could be used as successfully in the winter months.

Since most cheesecake and gâteaux recipes are labour intensive, they do not make ideal same-day-of-eating desserts. You can, however, stagger their preparation over several days, making sponge layers, meringue discs, cheesecake bases, fruity fillings and special decorations well ahead.

For this reason cheesecakes and gâteaux make welcome additions to cook-ahead menus featuring other prepared-in-advance starter and main course standbys such as jellied game pâtés or terrines, soups, savoury egg or fish mousses and marinated vegetable salads. Pasta and rice dishes that simply need reheating or completing, casseroles, hot pots, curries and other spicy dishes that welcome the chance to mature in the refrigerator for a day are good main course selections.

From the left: Lime Cheesecake (page 140), Strawberry and Orange Gâteau (page 143)

Opposite: Strawberry Cheesecake Gâteau

STRAWBERRY CHEESECAKE GÂTEAU

Preparation time: 45 minutes, plus setting
Cooking time: 20 minutes
Oven: 180°C, 350°F, Gas Mark 4
Serves 4-6

Sponge base:
50 g (2 oz) soft margarine at room temperature
50 g (2 oz) self-raising flour, sifted
½ teaspoon baking powder
1 egg
50 g (2 oz) caster sugar
225 g (8 oz) strawberries
Cheesecake filling:
350 g (12 oz) curd cheese
75 g (3 oz) caster sugar
15 g (½ oz) powdered gelatine
3 tablespoons water
1 teaspoon vanilla essence
200 ml (⅓ pint) double or whipping cream, whipped
3 egg whites, stiffly whisked
To decorate:
1 tablespoon sifted icing sugar
85 ml (3 fl oz) double or whipping cream, stiffly whipped

1. Grease and line an 18 cm (7 inch) sandwich tin. Place the margarine, flour, baking powder, egg and sugar in a mixing bowl and whisk until light and fluffy. Cook in a preheated oven for 20 minutes. Turn out on to a wire tray to cool.
2. Mix the curd cheese with the caster sugar. Dissolve the gelatine in the water over a gentle heat and add to the cheese with the vanilla essence. Fold in the whipped cream. Lightly fold the whisked egg whites into the cheese mixture.
3. Lightly oil the sides of a 16 cm (6½ inch) loose-based cake tin. Cut the sponge in half horizontally and place the bottom half in the tin.
4. Reserving 6 strawberries for decoration, slice the rest on to the sponge base. Pour in the cheesecake mixture and top with the reserved sponge. Chill until set.
5. When set, carefully remove from the tin. Dust the top with sifted icing sugar. Decorate with whirls of cream and the reserved strawberries.

Variations: Cheesecakes make a very versatile dessert with many variations. There are many types of soft cheese now on the market and most are suitable for cheesecakes. Curd cheese, cottage cheese if sieved and skimmed milk soft cheese are all good for keeping the calories down. If full-fat soft cheese is used, half the cream in the recipe can be replaced by plain unsweetened yogurt.

The strawberries in the recipe can be replaced by any other soft fruit or to make a lemon cheesecake omit the vanilla essence and add the grated rind and juice of 2 lemons but add a further ½ teaspoon of powdered gelatine.

If a biscuit crumb base is preferred rather than the sponge base, crumble 175 g (6 oz) digestive biscuits, mix with 50 g (2 oz) caster sugar with 50 g (2 oz) melted butter. Put half the mixture into the base of the tin then sprinkle the rest over the top.

GÂTEAU ST HONORÉ

Preparation time: 1 hour plus chilling, cooling and infusing
Cooking time: 1½ hours
Oven: Base: 180°C, 350°F, Gas Mark 4.
Choux paste: 230°C, 450°F, Gas Mark 8; then 190°C, 375°F, Gas Mark 5
Serves 8

Pastry base:
100 g (4 oz) plain flour
pinch of salt
50 g (2 oz) butter
25 g (1 oz) vanilla sugar
1 egg yolk
Choux paste:
50 g (2 oz) butter
150 ml (¼ pint) water
65 g (2½ oz) plain flour
pinch of salt
2 eggs, beaten
Filling:
450 ml (¾ pint) double or whipping cream, whipped
Glaze:
225 g (8 oz) sugar
150 ml (¼ pint) water
Crème St Honoré:
300 ml (½ pint) milk
1 vanilla pod
1 egg and 1 egg yolk
50 g (2 oz) caster sugar
20 g (¾ oz) plain flour
15 g (½ oz) cornflour
15 g (½ oz) butter
2 egg whites, stiffly beaten
To decorate:
glacé fruit
angelica

This gâteau is named after the patron saint of pastry cooks and bakers. The pastry base and the choux ring and buns can be made in advance, but the gâteau must be eaten the same day it is filled.

1. Make the pastry base: sift the flour with the salt on to a work surface. Make a well in the centre, add the butter and sugar and work together with the fingertips of one hand.

2. Add the egg yolk and mix to a soft dough with the heel of one hand. Wrap in clingfilm and chill for 30 minutes.

3. Roll out the dough to a 21 cm (8½ inch) round. Place on a baking sheet, prick with a fork and crimp the edge with the fingers. Bake for about 20 minutes in a preheated oven, until light golden. Cool on the baking sheet until beginning to firm, then transfer carefully to a wire rack and leave to cool completely.

4. Meanwhile, place the butter and water for the choux paste in a saucepan and melt over low heat. Sift the flour with the salt on to a sheet of greaseproof paper.

5. Bring the butter and water mixture in the pan to the boil, remove from the heat and tip the flour quickly into the pan. Beat with a wooden spoon until the mixture forms a paste and leaves the sides of the pan clean. (Do not overbeat or the mixture will become oily.) Allow to cool until tepid.

6. Gradually add the eggs, beating hard between each addition until the paste is glossy and of a smooth piping consistency.

7. Grease and flour two baking sheets. Press the rim of a 21 cm (8½ inch) flan ring on one of the baking sheets, to make an imprint. Remove the ring.

8. Spoon the choux paste into a piping bag fitted with a large plain nozzle. Using the floured ring as a guide, pipe two-thirds of the paste in a circle on the baking sheet.

9. With the remaining choux, pipe out 12 small buns on to the second baking sheet. Bake the buns and the ring in a preheated oven for 15 minutes, then reduce the oven and bake for a further 20 minutes, or until puffed and golden.

10. Pierce the bases of the buns and the ring to release the steam and cool on a wire rack. Split the choux ring when cold and use a teaspoon to scoop out any soggy or uncooked pastry.

11. Meanwhile, place the milk and vanilla pod for the Crème St Honoré in a saucepan and bring just to the boil. Remove from heat and leave to infuse for 30 minutes, then discard the vanilla pod.

12. To make the glaze, dissolve the sugar with the water over gentle heat, then bring to the boil and boil rapidly to 127°C, 260°F or until a caramel colour. Using tongs, dip the tops and sides of the buns into the syrup and leave on a rack to harden.

13. Place the pastry base on a serving plate, position the choux ring base on top and pipe whipped cream into the base. Replace the top of the choux ring and arrange the glazed buns on top of the ring, dipping your fingers in iced water so that the syrup does not stick.

14. To make the Crème St Honoré, cream the egg and yolk, sugar, flour and cornflour together. Reheat the vanilla-flavoured milk and pour on to the mixture. Mix well, then return to the pan and bring to the boil, stirring continuously, until the mixture thickens. Boil gently for 2-3 minutes, then stir in the butter until melted. Allow to cool, then fold in the egg whites and spoon into the centre of the pastry ring.

15. Decorate the completed Gâteau St Honoré with small and colourful glacé fruits and angelica.

Gâteau St Honoré

BLACK CHERRY GÂTEAU

Preparation time: 20-25 minutes, plus cooling
Cooking time: 20-25 minutes
Oven: 190°C, 375°F, Gas Mark 5
Serves 6-8

225 g (8 oz) butter or hard margarine
225 g (8 oz) caster sugar
4 eggs
225 g (8 oz) self-raising flour, sifted
pinch of salt
2 tablespoons hot water
Filling:
50 g (2 oz) soft margarine
100 g (4 oz) icing sugar
½ tablespoon cocoa powder
½ tablespoon hot water
Topping:
1 × 450 g (16 oz) can pitted black cherries, drained
450 ml (¾ pint) whipping cream
40 g (1½ oz) plain chocolate, grated

1. Grease two 23 cm (9 inch) round sandwich cake tins and line the bases with greased greaseproof paper.
2. In a bowl, beat together the butter or margarine and sugar until light and fluffy. Add the eggs one at a time, beating well after each addition.
3. Add the flour with the salt and gently fold into the mixture, using a large metal spoon. Fold in the hot water, to give a fairly soft dropping consistency.
4. Divide the mixture evenly between the tins and smooth the surfaces. Bake in a preheated oven for 20-25 minutes until golden brown, cooked through and springy to the touch.
5. Turn the cakes on to a wire rack, carefully remove the lining papers and leave to cool completely. [A] [F]
6. Meanwhile to make the filling, beat together the margarine and icing sugar until smooth. Blend the cocoa powder with the hot water and add to the mixture. Beat thoroughly until the mixture is smooth and evenly blended. [A]
7. Reserve 40 cherries for the topping and roughly chop the remainder. Add the chopped cherries to the buttercream and mix well.
8. Spread the top of one of the cooled cakes with the buttercream mixture. Place the remaining cake on top.
9. Whip the cream stiffly and use half of it to spread over the top and sides of the gâteau. Place the remaining cream in a piping bag fitted with a large star nozzle. Coat the sides of the gâteau with the grated chocolate, reserving a little for decorating the finished gâteau.
10. Pipe a decorative border of cream around the top of the cake and arrange the reserved cherries inside the border. Pipe the remaining cream into swirls or rosettes in the centre of the gâteau and sprinkle with the remaining grated chocolate.

[A] Sandwich cakes can be prepared the previous day and stored in an airtight tin.
[F] Freeze for up to 3 months. Thaw for 3 hours at room temperature before following instructions given from step 6.
[M] Or microwave on Defrost for 2-4 minutes, then stand for 5 minutes. Defrost the layers separately, before following instructions from step 6.

Opposite: *Black Cherry Gâteau*

NECTARINE VACHERIN

Preparation time: 30 minutes
Cooking time: 1-1¼ hours
Oven: 140°C, 275°F, Gas Mark 1
Serves 12-14

50 g (2 oz) hazelnuts, toasted
6 egg whites
350 g (12 oz) caster sugar
450 ml (15 fl oz) whipping cream, whipped
6 nectarines, stoned and sliced

Dried out meringues will store well for several months in a cool dry place. Wrap in foil or store in a rigid plastic container.
1. Grind or grate the hazelnuts.
2. Draw a 23 cm (9 inch) circle on each of 3 pieces of non-stick silicone paper or greaseproof paper. Place the paper on baking sheets. Lightly oil the greaseproof paper.
3. Using a scrupulously clean and dry bowl and whisk, whisk the egg whites until stiff, then whisk in the sugar, a tablespoon at a time, until stiff and glossy. Fold in the prepared hazelnuts with a metal spoon.
4. Spread the hazelnut meringue (or pipe with a large plain nozzle) over the 3 circles.
5. Bake in a preheated oven for 1-1¼ hours until crisp and dry. Leave to cool, then peel off the paper.
6. Layer the meringue rounds with whipped cream and nectarines, decorating the top with cream and nectarines.

LIME CHEESECAKE

Preparation time: 25 minutes, plus cooling and chilling
Serves 4-6

Base:
75 g (3 oz) digestive biscuits, finely crushed
40 g (1½ oz) butter, melted
25 g (1 oz) demerara sugar
Filling:
1 × 600 ml (1 pint) lime jelly tablet
grated rind and juice of 1 lime
225 g (8 oz) cottage cheese, sieved
150 ml (¼ pint) double cream
1 tablespoon caster sugar
To decorate:
double or whipping cream, whipped
candied angelica leaves

This is a very light cheesecake. For a special occasion a richer version could be made using full fat soft cheese.
1. Mix together the biscuit crumbs, butter and sugar. Press evenly over the bottom of an 18 cm (7 inch) diameter flan tin or ring standing on a baking sheet. Chill.
2. To make the filling, make up the jelly to 300 ml (½ pint) with boiling water. Stir until completely dissolved. Add the lime rind and juice. Chill until nearly set.
3. Mix the cottage cheese with the cream. Stir in the jelly and sugar until smooth and well blended (using a blender, if liked).
4. Pour into the flan tin and chill until set. [F]
5. Pipe the whipped cream for the decoration in rosettes on a flat sheet and chill to set. [F]
6. To serve, place the rosettes on top of the cheesecake and decorate them with the angelica leaves. Serve chilled.

[F] Open freeze the rosettes and cheesecake. Put the frozen cream rosettes into a rigid freezer container and cover. When the cheesecake is solid, wrap it. Freeze both. Allow the cheesecake to thaw in the refrigerator for 4 hours. Place the rosettes on top and thaw for 2 more hours.

Opposite: Nectarine Vacherin

Illustrated on page 132

TRADITIONAL BAKED CHEESECAKE

Preparation time: 30 minutes, plus chilling
Cooking time: 180°C, 350°F, Gas Mark 4
Serves 8

175 g (6 oz) plain flour
pinch of salt
40 g (1½ oz) butter or margarine
40 g (1½ oz) lard
about 2 tablespoons water
½ egg white, stirred
Filling:
50 g (2 oz) butter or margarine
50 g (2 oz) caster sugar
450 g (1 lb) curd cheese
2 grade 1 or 2 eggs, beaten
100 g (4 oz) seedless raisins
25 g (1 oz) ground almonds
finely grated rind and juice of 1 lemon
25 g (1 oz) demerara sugar

1. To make the pastry, sift the flour and salt into a bowl. Add the butter or margarine and lard in pieces, then rub into the flour until the mixture resembles fine breadcrumbs. Stir in the water gradually and mix to a firm dough.
2. Roll out the dough on a lightly floured surface and use it to line an 18 cm (7 inch) loose-bottomed springform tin. Trim and flute the edge, then brush all over the dough with the egg white. Chill.
3. To make the filling, put the butter or margarine and sugar in a bowl and cream together until light and fluffy. Add the curd cheese and beat until soft. Beat in the remaining ingredients one at a time, except the demerara sugar.
4. Spoon the filling into the pastry-lined pan, then sprinkle with the demerara sugar. Stand the tin on a baking sheet, then bake in the oven for 50 minutes or until the filling is set. Remove the tin carefully from the sides of the cheesecake and return to the oven for a further 10 minutes until the pastry is golden. Remove from the oven and leave until cold.

Traditional Baked Cheesecake

STRAWBERRY AND ORANGE GÂTEAU

Preparation time: 30 minutes
Cooking time: 10 minutes
Oven: 220°C, 425°F, Gas Mark 7
Serves 6

3 eggs
75 g (3 oz) caster sugar, warmed
75 g (3 oz) self-raising flour
1 tablespoon hot water
Buttercream:
100 g (4 oz) butter, softened
225 g (8 oz) icing sugar, sifted
grated rind of 1 orange
2 tablespoons orange juice
To serve:
150 ml (¼ pint) double cream
225 g (8 oz) fresh or frozen strawberries
2-3 tablespoons redcurrant jelly, melted

Illustrated on page 132

1. Grease and line a 28×18 cm (11×7 inch) Swiss roll tin.
2. Break the eggs into a bowl. Add the sugar and whisk until thick, pale and the whisk leaves a trail when lifted.
3. Sift the flour over the whisked mixture and fold in with a metal spoon. Add the hot water.
4. Spoon the mixture into the prepared tin and spread evenly. Bake in a preheated oven for 10 minutes or until risen, golden and springy to touch.
5. Turn out on to a sheet of non-stick silicone paper. Leave the lining paper on the cake, cover with a damp tea towel and leave to cool.
6. Beat together the butter, icing sugar, orange rind and juice until blended, smooth and soft.
7. Remove the towel and paper from the sponge. Trim the crusty edges from the sides of the sponge, then cut into four equal strips lengthways. Spread each strip with the buttercream.
8. Take one strip of sponge, stand it on its edge and curl it round into a spiral with the iced side in. Join the next strip of sponge to the end of the first and continue to wind round, using the remaining strips to complete the spiral. [F]
9. Whip the cream and spread half over the side of the cake. Cover the top with the strawberries (thawed if frozen) and brush with the melted redcurrant jelly to glaze. Pipe the top decoratively with the remaining cream. Serve chilled.

[F] Open freeze, then wrap and store. To serve, allow to thaw for 2 hours in the refrigerator then complete the recipe from step 9.

*Chilled Mandarin
Cheesecake*

CHILLED MANDARIN CHEESECAKE

Preparation time: 30 minutes, plus chilling
Serves 8

Base
175 g (6 oz) digestive biscuits
50 g (2 oz) shelled hazelnuts or walnuts,
finely chopped
100 g (4 oz) butter, melted
Filling
1 × 350 g (12 oz) can mandarins
1 sachet (1 tablespoon) powdered gelatine
finely grated rind and juice of 1 lemon
350 g (12 oz) full-fat soft cheese
150 ml (¼ pint) soured cream
75 g (3 oz) caster sugar
2 eggs, separated

1. Crush the biscuits in an electric blender or between 2 sheets of greaseproof paper. Mix them with the chopped nuts and melted butter, then press into the base of a buttered loose-bottomed 20 cm (8 inch) springform pan. Chill in the refrigerator for about 30 minutes until firm.
2. Meanwhile, drain and reserve the mandarins and measure 150 ml (¼ pint) juice. Sprinkle the gelatine over the juice in a small heatproof bowl, then leave until spongy. Stand the bowl in a pan of hot water and heat gently until the gelatine has dissolved, stirring occasionally. Remove from the heat, stir in the lemon rind and juice, then leave until cold.
3. Put the cheese, soured cream and sugar in a bowl and beat together until soft, then stir in the egg yolks until evenly blended. Stir in the cooled gelatine liquid.
4. Beat the egg whites until stiff, then fold in the cream cheese mixture. Pour into the biscuit-lined pan, then chill in the refrigerator overnight until set. Remove the cheesecake from the pan, place on a serving platter and decorate with the reserved mandarin oranges. Serve chilled.

CHERRY GÂTEAU CARDINALE

Preparation time: 40 minutes
Cooking time: 30-35 minutes
Oven: 180°C, 350°F, Gas Mark 4
Serves 4-6

100 g (4 oz) soft margarine, at room temperature
100 g (4 oz) self-raising flour
100 g (4 oz) caster sugar
2 eggs, beaten
1 teaspoon baking powder
½ teaspoon almond essence
300 ml (½ pint) double or whipping cream, whipped
100 g (4 oz) ripe red cherries, stoned and halved
50 g (2 oz) flaked almonds, toasted
100 g (4 oz) redcurrant jelly

1. Grease and line two 18 cm (7 inch) sandwich tins.
2. Put the margarine, flour, sugar, eggs, baking powder and almond essence in a mixing bowl and whisk for 2-3 minutes until the mixture is light and fluffy.
3. Divide the mixture between the 2 tins. Bake in a preheated oven for 30-35 minutes. Turn the cakes out on to a wire tray to cool.
4. Mix half the cream with the cherries and use to sandwich the cakes together.
5. Spread a little of the remaining cream around the side of the gâteau and either press the almonds on to the cream, using a palette knife, or place the almonds on a chopping board and roll the cake in them to coat.
6. Melt the redcurrant jelly in a pan over a gentle heat. Whisk until smooth. Cool until almost set, then pour over the top within 1 cm (½ inch) of the edge.
7. Put the remaining cream into a piping bag with a star nozzle and pipe around the edge of the redcurrant jelly.

Cherry Gâteau Cardinale

ICES & SORBETS

Sliced thickly on to plates; scooped and piled high in glasses; or lavishly layered on sponge, fruit or wafers – few ice creams and sorbets can ever be refused.

Once rare treats or special occasion desserts made only from the finest cream, eggs and fruit, home-made ice creams and sorbets are now available to everyone with a freezing compartment in their refrigerator.

Ices and sorbets are very versatile desserts, taking on a host of guises and flavours according to their ingredients. A basic vanilla ice cream recipe can be creamy smooth and mild in flavour, yet quickly made crunchy, richer and chocolatey by the addition of just one ingredient. Add more spices, fruits, flavourings like citrus zest and real fruit essences, chopped nuts, chopped herbs or liqueurs or spirits and you have the basis for a whole new repertoire of ice creams to be enjoyed.

The same can be said for the often simpler water ice or sorbet. The addition of more egg white, more or less fruit, a sprinkling of fruit juice or more than a splash of wine takes it to new heights of extra smoothness, stronger colour and flavour and menu suitability.

Ices and sorbets are also the best friend of the quick cook, busy hostess and impromptu chef. Stashed away in the freezer, they often need little extra attention for serving beyond perhaps a stab with a crisp biscuit or wafer, a sprinkling of nuts, a swirl of cream, a dusting of spices or the decorative prettiness of a sprig of fresh mint.

These are the ideal desserts to serve after a hot starter like a meat broth, baked eggs, miniature meat or fish kebabs or individual hot vegetable tartlets or quiches. They are almost compulsory after an extra-hot main course like a curry, peppery goulash like Hungarian, Chilli con Carne or a peppercorn- or mustard-coated steak of fish or meat. Remember to serve light sorbets when the weight has featured strongly at the forefront of the meal and richer, creamier offerings when appetites need satisfying.

From the top: Tangerine Dreams (page 151), Peach Ice Cream (page 148)

Vanilla Ice Cream

VANILLA ICE CREAM

Preparation: 20 minutes, plus cooling and freezing
Cooking time: 10-15 minutes
Serves 6-8

3 egg yolks
100 g (4 oz) vanilla sugar
250 ml (8 fl oz) milk
300 ml (½ pint) double cream

1. Whisk the yolks and sugar until white and creamy. Heat the milk to simmering point and pour over the yolks. Mix well.
2. Pour the custard into the rinsed pan and heat until it coats the back of a wooden spoon. Pour into a bowl and cool.
3. Whisk the double cream until it thickens, then fold into the custard.
4. Pour the custard into a freezer container and place in the frezer. Freeze for about 2-3 hours or until it begins to set at the edge.
5. Remove the custard from the freezer and whisk thoroughly to break down the ice crystals. Return to the freezer for 1-2 hours or until firm.
6. If the ice cream has been in the freezer for 24 hours or longer, transfer to the refrigerator 15 minutes before serving.

PEACH ICE CREAM

Preparation time: 20 minutes, plus cooling and freezing
Cooking time: 15 minutes
Serves 6-8
4 large, ripe peaches, total weight about
750 g (1½ lb), skinned
50 g (2 oz) icing sugar
1 tablespoon lemon juice
2 tablespoons white wine
2 teaspoons gelatine
4 egg yolks
300 ml (½ pint) double cream

Illustrated on page 146

1. Purée the peach flesh with the sugar.
2. Mix together the lemon juice and wine in a bowl and sprinkle on the gelatine.
3. Transfer the peach purée to a heatproof bowl. Beat in the egg yolks. Place the bowl over a pan of gently simmering water and stir until it thickens slightly.
4. Put the bowl of gelatine mixture into a shallow pan of hot water and leave until it dissolves. Stir the gelatine into the peach mixture and leave to cool.
5. Whip the cream until it forms soft peaks then fold it into the mixture. Transfer it to a freezer container. Freeze until firm, beating twice at hourly intervals. **[F]**

[F] Freeze for 6 months.

CHAMPAGNE WATER-ICE

Preparation time: 15 minutes, plus freezing
Serves 6

225 g (8 oz) sugar
300 ml (½ pint) water
300 ml (½ pint) champagne
juice of 1 lemon and 1 orange

A water-ice is quick and simple to make, being basically a sugar syrup flavoured with fruit juice and then frozen. The addition of alcohol means that the ice will melt very quickly at room temperature, so leave it in the freezer until just before serving.

1. Set the freezer to coldest. If making the water-ice without a processor or sorbetière, put a bowl and whisk into the freezer to chill. If using a processor for the whisking, freeze the mixture in ice-cube trays and when rock-solid, process the cubes to smoothness.

2. Dissolve the sugar in the water. Add the champagne and fruit juices. Pour into shallow trays and freeze. When frozen round the edges but still soft in the centre, tip into the chilled bowl and whisk until smooth. Refreeze.

3. Repeat the whisking at intervals until creamy, smooth and white.

4. Chill serving glasses or bowls before dinner.

Champagne Water-Ice

STRAWBERRY BAKED ALASKA

Preparation time: 10 minutes, plus soaking
Cooking time: 3 minutes
Oven: 230°C, 450°F, Gas Mark 8
Serves 6

about 350 g (¾ lb) fresh strawberries,
hulled and sliced
4-6 tablespoons Marsala or sweet sherry
3 egg whites
100 g (4 oz) caster sugar
1 × 20 cm (8 inch) sponge flan case
450 ml (¾ pint) Vanilla ice cream
(see page 148)

Baked Alaska always makes an impressive dinner party dessert, but it does have to be prepared at the last minute or the ice cream will melt. To make things easier, however, it can be made in advance up until baking, then frozen until solid. To serve, bake from frozen for about 5 minutes until thawed.

1. Put the strawberries in a bowl, sprinkle over half the Marsala or sherry, then leave to marinate.

2. Meanwhile, beat the egg whites until stiff, fold in the sugar, then beat again until glossy. Set aside. Stand the flan case on a heatproof serving platter and sprinkle over the remaining Marsala or sherry.

3. Pile the macerated strawberries in the flan case. Soften the ice cream slightly, then spread it over the strawberries in a dome shape. Spoon the meringue mixture quickly over the ice cream and flan case to cover them completely, then bake immediately in the oven for about 3 minutes until the meringue is lightly browned. Serve immediately.

Strawberry Baked Alaska

TANGERINE DREAMS

Preparation time: 35 minutes, plus cooling and freezing
Cooking time: 15-20 minutes
Serves 6

8 large, loose-skinned tangerines or
satsumas
1 tablespoon lemon juice
1 egg and 1 extra yolk
100 g (4 oz) caster sugar
300 ml (½ pint) double or whipping cream
evergreen leaves, to decorate

If you have any ice cream left over after filling the tangerine cups, store it in the freezer for another time.

1. Finely grate the rind from 2 of the tangerines. Cut off the tops from the remaining 6 tangerines and reserve. Using a curved grapefruit knife or a sharp-edged teaspoon, scoop out the tangerine flesh.

2. Put the flesh into a strainer and press out the juice. Measure the juice and if it is less then 300 ml (½ pint), make it up to this quantity by squeezing the juice from the 2 tangerines whose skins you have grated. $\boxed{A}$ Pour the juice into a small heavy-based saucepan. Add the lemon juice and bring the juices to the boil.

3. Meanwhile, put the egg, the extra yolk and the sugar into a heatproof bowl and beat until the mixture is thick and pale.

4. Pour the boiling juice on to the egg mixture in a thin stream, beating all the time. Place the bowl over a pan of boiling water and stir until the mixture thickens to a custard. Leave to cool, then chill in the refrigerator.

5. Whip the cream until it forms soft peaks, then fold it into the chilled custard. Transfer the mixture to a freezer container, cover and freeze, beating twice at hourly intervals. $\boxed{F}$

6. Arrange the tangerine shells on a baking sheet and chill thoroughly in the refrigerator.

7. Two hours before serving, transfer the ice cream to the refrigerator to soften for 35-40 minutes. Using a metal spoon fill the shells with ice cream and replace the tops. Brush the skins with cold water to frost them and return them to the freezer.

8. 10 minutes before serving, transfer the tangerines to the refrigerator. Serve the tangerines on a large dish, strewn with glossy evergreen leaves.

$\boxed{A}$ Prepare the tangerine cups and the juice the day before and keep in the refrigerator.
$\boxed{F}$ Freeze for 6 months.

Illustrated on page 146

STRAWBERRY ICE CREAM

Preparation time: 15 minutes, plus freezing
Serves 6

450 g (1 lb) fresh strawberries, hulled
4 tablespoons fresh orange juice
175 g (6 oz) caster sugar
450 ml (¾ pint) whipping cream

1. Mash the strawberries finely and mix with the orange juice to form a smooth purée. Stir in the sugar.
2. Whip the cream until soft peaks form and fold into the strawberry purée.
3. Pour the mixture into a 1 kg (2 lb) loaf tin. Cover and freeze for 1½ hours or until partly frozen.
4. Turn the mixture into a bowl, break it up with a fork and whisk until smooth. Return the mixture to the loaf tin and freeze for at least a further 5 hours until completely frozen. **F**
5. Transfer the ice cream to the main compartment of the refrigerator for 25-30 minutes before required for serving, to soften lightly. Serve with fan wafers.

F Freeze for up to 3 months.

VANILLA AND BLACKCURRANT RIPPLE ICE

Preparation time: 15 minutes, plus freezing
Cooking time: 2-3 minutes
Serves 4-5

150 ml (¼ pint) single cream
3 egg yolks
40-50 g (1½-2 oz) caster sugar
1 teaspoon vanilla essence
300 ml (½ pint) whipping cream
2 tablespoons blackcurrant jelly preserve

1. Heat the single cream until hot but not boiling. Place the egg yolks in a heatproof bowl and mix with a fork.
2. Pour the hot cream on to the egg yolks, stirring all the time. Stir in the sugar and vanilla essence. Place the bowl over a saucepan of gently simmering water and stir for about 8-10 minutes with a wooden spoon until the mixture thickens and coats the back of the spoon. Strain into a bowl and leave to cool.
3. Whip the whipping cream until soft peaks form and lightly fold into the custard, using a large metal spoon.
4. Turn the mixture into a 1 kg (2 lb) loaf tin, cover and freeze for 1½ hours or until partly frozen.
5. Warm the blackcurrant jelly in a saucepan until smooth and melted. Leave to cool but do not allow to set. Meanwhile, turn the ice cream into a bowl, break up with a fork and whisk until smooth.
6. Return the mixture to the loaf tin. Make 3 holes along the centre of the ice cream and pour in the melted blackcurrant jelly. Run a knife through the jelly and ice cream to give a marble effect.
7. Freeze for at least a further 4 hours until completely frozen. **F**
8. Transfer the ice cream to the main compartment of the refrigerator for 30 minutes before required for serving.

F Freeze for up to 3 months.

COFFEE PARFAIT

Preparation time: 15 minutes, plus chilling

3 teaspoons instant coffee powder
1 teaspoon drinking chocolate
2 teaspoons boiling water
¼ teaspoon vanilla essence
300 ml (½ pint) whipping cream
2 egg whites
50 g (2 oz) caster sugar
40 g (1½ oz) plain chocolate, grated

1. Dissolve the coffee and drinking chocolate in the boiling water, then leave to cool. Add the vanilla essence.
2. Whisk the cream until stiff and fold in the coffee and chocolate mixture, using a metal spoon.
3. Whisk the egg whites stiffly, then gradually add the sugar, whisking well after each addition until very stiff and glossy.
4. Lightly fold the egg whites and 25 g (1 oz) of the grated chocolate into the cream mixture, using a metal spoon.
5. Spoon the mixture into 6 individual serving dishes, sprinkle with the remaining grated chocolate and serve chilled, with fan wafers.

From the top:
Strawberry Ice Cream, Coffee Parfait, Vanilla and Blackcurrant Ripple Ice

From the left: Mango Ice Cream, Chocolate Chip Ice Cream

MANGO CREAM ICE

Preparation time: 15 minutes, plus cooling and freezing
Cooking time: 5-8 minutes
Serves 4-6

150 ml (¼ pint) single cream
3 egg yolks
75 g (3 oz) caster sugar
1 × 425 g (15 oz) can sliced mango in syrup, drained
200 ml (7 fl oz) double cream

1. Heat the single cream in a pan until just under boiling point. Put the egg yolks and sugar in a bowl and whisk well together.
2. Pour the hot cream on to the egg mixture, stirring well, then place the bowl over a pan of gently simmering water and whisk for 5-6 minutes until the mixture thickens to coat the back of a spoon.
3. Strain the mixture into a bowl and cool.
4. Purée the mango in a blender or food processor until smooth, then add to the custard mixture.
5. Whip the double cream until it forms soft peaks and fold into the mango custard, using a large metal spoon.
6. Pour the mixture into a freezer-proof container, cover and freeze until partially frozen around the edges. Using a fork, stir the frozen parts into the unfrozen parts until thoroughly combined, then cover and freeze until firm. [F]
7. About 20 minutes before required for serving, transfer the ice cream to the main compartment of the refrigerator to soften.
8. Slice, spoon or scoop the ice cream into serving dishes and serve with crisp wafers.

[F] Can be frozen for up to 3 months.

CHOCOLATE CHIP ICE CREAM

Preparation time: 15 minutes, plus cooling and freezing
Cooking time: 15 minutes
Serves 4-6

300 ml (½ pint) milk
75 g (3 oz) soft dark brown sugar
75 g (3 oz) plain chocolate, broken into pieces
2 eggs, beaten
½ teaspoon vanilla essence
300 ml (½ pint) double cream
75 g (3 oz) chocolate chips

1. Put the milk, sugar and chocolate in a pan and heat gently until the chocolate has melted and the sugar dissolved. Pour the warm mixture on to the beaten eggs, stirring all the time.
2. Return the mixture to the pan and cook over a low heat, stirring all the time, until the custard thickens very slightly. Strain the mixture into a bowl and add the vanilla essence. Cool.
3. Whip the cream until it forms soft peaks, then whisk into the cooled custard. Stir in the chocolate chips.
4. Turn the mixture into a freezer-proof container and freeze until firm. [F]
5. About 30 minutes before serving, transfer the container to the main compartment of the refrigerator to soften.
6. Slice, spoon or scoop the ice cream into serving dishes and serve.

[F] Can be frozen for up to 3 months.

RASPBERRY AND REDCURRANT SORBET

Preparation time: 20 minutes, plus freezing
Cooking time: 8 minutes
Serves 6

225 g (8 oz) redcurrants, topped and tailed
225 g (8 oz) raspberries
300 ml (½ pint) cold water
175 g (6 oz) granulated sugar
1 tablespoon lemon juice
2 egg whites
To decorate:
sprigs of redcurrants (optional)

1. Put the redcurrants and raspberries into a saucepan with 150 ml (¼ pint) of the water and cook gently for 5 minutes. Cool slightly. Put the mixture into a blender or food processor, blend until smooth, then put through a nylon sieve.
2. Put the remaining water and the sugar in a small pan and heat gently, stirring to dissolve the sugar. Boil for 3 minutes. Remove from the heat, cool slightly, then add the fruit and lemon juice. Stir well.
3. Pour the mixture into a metal container and leave to cool. Freeze for 1-2 hours or until the mixture has set to a depth of 2.5 cm (1 inch) around the edges.
4. Turn the mixture into a bowl and break up with a fork, then whisk until smooth. Stiffly whisk the egg whites and lightly and evenly whisk them into the mixture.
5. Turn the mixture into a plastic container, cover and freeze for several hours or overnight, until firm. [F]
6. About 25-30 minutes before required for serving, transfer the sorbet to the main compartment of the refrigerator to soften slightly – it should be just firm enough to hold its shape when spooned or scooped.
7. Arrange in delicate glasses and decorate with redcurrant sprigs, if liked.

Illustrated on page 156

[F] Can be frozen for up to 3 months.

CRÈME DE MENTHE SORBET

Preparation time: 10 minutes, plus freezing
Cooking time: 12 minutes
Serves 8

1.2 litres (2 pints) cold water
450 g (1 lb) granulated sugar
8 sprigs of fresh mint
1 tablespoon lemon juice
5-6 tablespoons crème de menthe
2 egg whites
To decorate:
sprigs of fresh mint

1. Put the water and sugar into a large saucepan and heat gently, stirring to dissolve the sugar. Bring to the boil and boil for 5 minutes. Add the mint and boil for a further 5 minutes.
2. Stir in the lemon juice, cool for 30 minutes, then discard the mint.
3. Pour the mixture into a metal container and freeze for at least 6-8 hours or overnight until it is partially frozen.
4. Turn the mixture into a bowl and break up with a fork. Add the crème de menthe and whisk until smooth. Stiffly whisk the egg whites and whisk into the mixture.
5. Turn the mixture into a plastic container. Cover and freeze overnight until frozen but mushy-firm in texture, remembering that as this is a soft scoop sorbet it will not freeze solid. $\boxed{F}$
6. When required for serving, spoon or scoop the sorbet straight from the freezer. Serve decorated with sprigs of fresh mint.

$\boxed{F}$ Can be frozen for up to 3 months.

MANGO AND PASSION FRUIT SORBET

Preparation time: 20 minutes, plus freezing
Cooking time: 5 minutes
Serves 6

2 ripe mangoes
approx 450 ml (¾ pint) cold water
2 passion fruit
1 tablespoon lemon juice
150 g (5 oz) granulated sugar
2 egg whites

1. Halve and stone each mango. Scoop out the flesh, put into a blender and blend until smooth. Pour the mixture into a measuring jug and make up to 600 ml (1 pint) with water.
2. Halve the passion fruit and scoop out the contents into the mango mixture. Add the lemon juice and stir well.
3. Put 150 ml (¼ pint) of the remaining water in a small saucepan with the sugar. Heat slowly, stirring to dissolve the sugar. Boil for 3 minutes. Remove from the heat, cool, add the mango mixture. Pass the mixture through a nylon sieve.
4. Pour the mixture into a metal container and leave to cool. Freeze for 1-2 hours or until the mixture has set to a depth of 2.5 cm (1 inch) around the edges.
5. Turn the mixture into a bowl and break it up with a fork, then whisk until smooth. Stiffly whisk the egg whites and lightly and evenly whisk into the mixture.
6. Turn the mixture into a plastic container, cover and freeze for several hours or overnight, until firm. $\boxed{F}$
7. About 25-30 minutes before required, transfer the sorbet to the refrigerator to soften slightly. Serve with crisp biscuits.

$\boxed{F}$ Can be frozen for up to 3 months.

From the top: Raspberry and Redcurrant Sorbet (page 155), Crème de Menthe Sorbet, Mango with Passion Fruit Sorbet

INDEX

ACKNOWLEDGEMENTS

The following photographs were taken specially for this book:
Vernon Morgan: 2-3, 4-5, 6, 18, 20, 30, 34, 46, 62, 70, 82, 91, 92, 104, 115, 118, 156. Stylist: Rebecca Gillies.
Food prepared for photography by Nicola Diggins and Hilary Foster.
Illustrations by Nadine Wickenden and Charlie Wess.
Cover photography: Vernon Morgan.

The following photographs were taken specially for Octopus Books Ltd:
Bryce Attwell: 66, 116, 142, 144, 150-1; Phillip Dowell: 148; Laurie Evans: 8, 11, 23, 29, 36, 39, 40, 45, 51, 55, 56,
58, 60, 65, 73, 89, 94, 96-7, 101, 103, 107, 109, 111, 125, 126-7, 131, 135, 139, 141, 145, 153; Robert Golden: 74-5, 81;
Melvyn Grey: 43; Christine Hanscomb: 32, 121, 122, 149; Gina Harris: 25; James Jackson: 14, 17, 49, 69, 79;
Vernon Morgan: 13, 86-7, 113, 137, 154; Peter Myers: 26, 53, 77, 128-9, 132; Ian O'Leary: 84, 85, 146; Charlie
Stebbings: 99.

Some of the recipes in this book previously appeared in the following books published by Octopus Books
Ltd:
Appetizing Starters, Chinese Cooking, The Cookery Year, Cooking for the Family (Louise Steele), Cooking for
the Family (Rosemary Wadey), Cooking for Your Freezer, Delicious Desserts, The Encyclopedia of Desserts,
The Encyclopedia of Italian Cooking, Four Seasons Salads, French Bistro Cookery, French Cooking, The Herb
Book, Just Desserts, St Michael Cookery Course, Summer Desserts, Sweet Success, Traditional British
Cooking, Vegetarian Feast, The Wholefood Cookbook.

The publishers would like to thank the following for lending items used in the photography for this book:
Harrods Limited, Knightsbridge, London SW1X 7XL; David Mellor, 26 James Street, Covent Garden, London
WC2E 8PA.